Single PAST 50

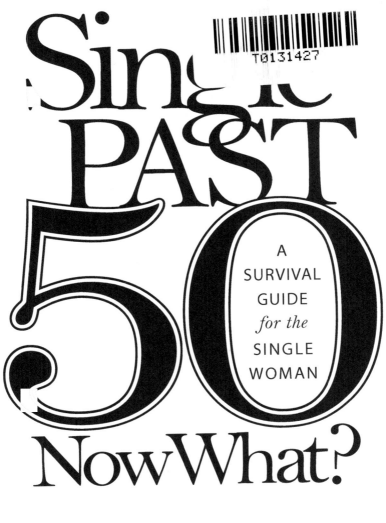

A SURVIVAL GUIDE *for the* SINGLE WOMAN

Now What?

TAMMY BLECK

MORGAN JAMES PUBLSHING • NEW YORK

Single PAST 50 Now What?

Copyright ©2008 Tammy Bleck

ISBN: 978-1-60037-370-1 (Paperback)
Library of Congress Control Number: 2007941186

This publication is designed to provide accurate and authoritative information with regard to the subject matter covered. It is sold with the understanding that the publisher is not engaged in rendering legal, accounting, or other professional advice. If legal advice or other expert assistance is required, the services of a competent professional person should be sought. Many of the designations used by manufacturers and sellers to distinguish their products are claimed as trademarks. Where those designations appear in this book and Morgan James was aware of a trademark claim, the designations have been printed with initial capital letters.

Published by:

MORGAN · JAMES
THE ENTREPRENEURIAL PUBLISHER™
www.morganjamespublishing.com

Morgan James Publishing, LLC
1225 Franklin Ave Ste 32
Garden City, NY 11530-1693
Toll Free 800-485-4943
www.MorganJamesPublishing.com

Cover/Interior Design by:
Rachel Campbell
rachel@r2cdesign.com

Habitat for Humanity®
Peninsula Building Partner

Note to Readers

Fasten your seat belts.
It's going to be a bumpy night.

- from *All About Eve*, screenplay
by JOSEPH LEO MANKIEWICZ

◆✦ **NO KIDDING.** For those of us who are over fifty, truer words were never spoken. Many of us have lived beyond our happily ever after, have lost someone close to us, watched our kids leave the nest, experienced insecurities of huge proportions, gained weight, lost weight, gained it again, have been cheated on or have been unfaithful to, have lost jobs, lost friends, lost hope, lost direction, lost love. In short, growing old is a bitch. Many of the women who came before us can show us the way. In the words of another famous dame:

The hardest years are the ones between 10 and 70.

- HELEN HAYES

To Amanda. You are my sunshine.

Acknowledgements

◆◆ **IT'S HARD TO KNOW** what you want to be when you grow up. I'm actually still working on the prospect of becoming something, someday. While I eagerly try new things, think up silly ideas, go for broke (literally), it has been my daughter Amanda and my handful of friends who have helped me believe that I'm okay just the way I am. That's a big deal in my book.

My dear sweet Amanda, whom I want so much to never disappoint, and who has always been my reason for so many things, I wonder if you will ever know how much you inspire me to try to be worthy of your admiration and love. I am so very proud of you. And yes, I really do want to be just like you when I grow up.

Life can be tough. If it were not for my friends and family, it would sometimes be almost unbearable. Tia, Cynthia, Ron, Nancy, and Miss Gertrude, I'm so appreciative of your belief in me. I love you and I hope to someday live up to your expectations.

Papa, I'm grateful for you. Yes, we did make up for lost time, and the proof was in the pudding after all. Thank you for your never-ending confidence in my abilities and for your amazing optimism. I am proud to be a chip off the old block.

Books don't write themselves, and they sure don't edit themselves. Dan and Joyce Miller proved to be a true thorn in my side. I am grateful for their astute eye and cooperative spirits. I wouldn't have wanted it any other way. And my dear friends, Pamela Weston and Anne Lefton, what saints you two are, and what a blessing you have been. Thank you for all your input and dedication; proof solid that good friends need not live close by to remain kindred spirits.

And finally I want to acknowledge and thank Rob, my ex husband. If we had not loved each other and married, I would have missed so much. Although I would classify you as a sure fire pain in the ass, you are my dearest friend, still. Thank you for our Amanda. Oh, and thank you for the divorce!

Table of Contents

Introduction

◆✦ **WHAT HAPPENS WHEN** you get 100 single women past 50 in a room and have them take a survey on the happiness or unhappiness of their singlehood? Their honest answers clearly defined for me what I believe is a new era: the happy UN-married mature single woman. Who knew?

Each woman was asked to explain why they were no longer married, how long they had been married, how many times they ventured into marriage, and who instigated the divorce. Each woman listed her life's priorities, hopes, fears, and aspirations.

Here's the clincher. Out of the 100 women surveyed, 98 emphatically stated that they did not wish to ever remarry.

What? Could it be possible that the mature woman past 50 is better off single? Yes, yes it is. The mature woman has stepped up and is setting the standard that defines her happily ever after; and it does NOT include a husband.

It's true that after divorce or death of a spouse, we often hit the skids. Some of us hit the pavement face first, spitting out the gravel as time goes by. Others hit the ground running. And all of us have difficulties to overcome, sadness to heal, anger to reconcile, and some pretty hefty problems to solve. As it turns out, we solve, we heal, we reconcile, and we come out of this life circumstance smarter, better, and stronger. That's not an opinion; it's a fact that presents itself over and over in the pages of this book.

You will not only be amazed by what you will learn, you will be left validated, rejuvenated, and redirected in your life and purpose.

If you are a mother, daughter, sister, aunt, or girlfriend who presently is or loves someone who is trying to survive singlehood or an unhappy marriage, these pages hold the answer to the question, "Am I better off single?" You tell me.

BEING SINGLE
PAST FIFTY

This is not the end.
It is not even the beginning of the end.
But, it is, perhaps, the end of the beginning.

- WINSTON CHURCHILL

S o you think that being single, in what are
supposed to be your golden years, is rough
and holds little promise for a happy future?
It could be because no one has ever bothered
to tell you that we single women have better sex, enjoy
stronger relationships, better friendships, get more rest, are

less depressed, travel more, have better bodies, and have less housework. Okay, I'll concede that it is rough going at first, but after you figure it out, honey, there is no holding you back from living an amazingly happy and fulfilled life. Chances are pretty good you won't want to remarry. Don't believe me? Then you need to read on. And pay attention!

We are going to turn your sorrows into excitement for the future. We are wise and wonderful women who know what it's like to feel confident, yet afraid. We have raised our children, but inside we don't feel much older ourselves. For all of us who still have a dance left in us, a hope still flickering, a chance to be more, this is our time. No one knows disappointment better, recognizes love easier, or practices patience more often. No one is more capable.

We are the ones who now understand that divorce does not mean failure, change does not foreshadow disaster, a few extra pounds does not equal ugly, passion and laughter often go hand and hand, and there is definitely life after 50. We cannot deny that we have fallen short of our own expectations, made wrong decisions, held grudges, and procrastinated ourselves into oblivion. Despite it all, we still try, still grow, still change, and still achieve, because we can.

What I'm about to tell you goes against everything you know or think you know. It goes against multi-million dollar industries that make sure you have the wrong idea - their idea. It goes against what your mother probably told you and what your family still expects of you. It may even go against your own thoughts and mind-set. Nevertheless, I believe it to be a solid truth: The woman over 50 often has little need for a husband, and is better off single.

To many of us, the appearance of the words "happily" and "single" in the same sentence presents us with an oxymoron. The actuality is—it's right on the mark. This is especially true for women over 50. If we can break free of the mold, the preconceived ideas that have been planted in us, we will realize a fuller, more wonderful life. Simply stated, for the woman over 50, life without a husband can be an amazing awakening and a life newly begun.

This book is not intended to dissuade anyone who has found wedded bliss. Rather, it addresses the woman who finds herself in the throes of singlehood, past the age of 50, and wondering if or when she should remarry. My advice would be to read these chapters carefully, gather the data, take inventory of your needs, and judge for yourself.

I'm not sure at what stage in our lives we were given the notion that our success and happiness depended on landing a man. Whatever age, whatever year it happened, it was a lie that has molded many of our lives, and not for the better.

Men, love, and relationships are all most wonderful things, and all those things can be experienced and lived by the mature single woman without the ties that bind called marriage. Whatever images have been conjured in our heads about "happily ever after" probably need adjusting.

Many single women have learned to embrace their freedoms, try new things; join their friends in social events, because three is not necessarily a crowd, but rather a gathering of friends. There is nothing we cannot do as single women. Life is short, and we have already lived half of it. It is time to get on with the business of making ourselves happy. This time around, ladies, it's all about us!

THE UNCOUPLE FACTOR

Choose well: your choice is brief and yet endless.

- ELLA WINTER

For the first time in our history married women are a minority. Go figure! Fifty-one percent of American women have chosen to live life without a spouse. Citing their preference for a more flexible lifestyle and greater independence, women choosing to be an uncouple have become the acceptable norm. It is a lifestyle achievement. One that has taken us decades to understand, accept and embrace. We get it now. We are single and happy about it. A lot happier than most of us thought we could be.

I don't know about you, but it gets a bit tiring to always be told that I can only be happy and complete when I find my soul mate. Especially offensive are the sappy diamond commercials that tell me that I will be happy and complete when a man proposes to me on the steps of a European landmark and gives me a diamond ring, and the hundreds of online dating services that tell me how much better my life will be when I find my perfect match. Enough already!

Marriage can be a wonderful thing when it works, but not all of us find ourselves basking in the glow of marital bliss. Let's get down to the nitty-gritty. If it's so rewarding being married, why are so many people choosing to stay single? Why is the divorce rate at 50% for first marriages and 75% for second marriages? And why has a new generation decided to wait until their late twenties to even consider making the leap for the first time?

It's no secret that we all want to have a special someone in our lives. Romance is alive and well in the mature, single woman. We are not anti-men, anti-romance, or anti-relationships. The contrary is true. Millions of women are discovering that while love and romance is a wanted and welcome component in their lives, there appears to be little evidence that marriage is always a benefit for the woman over fifty.

According to the 21st Edition of Statistics Abstract of the U.S., and the Statistics Handbook on the American Family, only one-half of married couples state that their relationships are happy. Hello? Are you listening? Divorce rates remain higher than they have been throughout most of this century. The number of people ending long-term marriages after age 50 is steadily increasing. They are shedding their marriages in the quest for happiness.

Anecdotal evidence suggests a growing trend. Several matrimonial lawyers in New York reported that they are having more clients 55 and older ending their marriages. There is a heavy concentration now of people over 50 who are divorcing. This mix is quite different from the one we have seen 10 or 15 years ago. Those who divorce later in life, whether they are in a first marriage or a subsequent one, cite many of the same triggers: infidelity, boredom, and drifting apart after children have left the home. The movement is clear. Many of our generation are looking at the prospect of many healthy years ahead of us, and we are opting to go it alone.

The Marriage and Family Therapy Program at the University of Minnesota states that part of the reason we are seeing a surge in divorce in those over 55 is that they are finding themselves not happy and not feeling fulfilled. This echoes recent research that found that among men and women 40 to 70 years of age, the wife usually initiates the divorce (Gibbs 2005).

I conducted interviews of 100 single women between the ages of 50 and 69. Each woman had been single for a minimum of three years. The topics discussed included: their fears and hopes, the ups and down of being single, sex, marriage, coupling, duration of marriage, initiator of the divorce, and number of children. Interestingly enough, only two of the 100 women interviewed stated they would like to remarry in the future. Only two! It was then I knew I was witnessing a new wave of single maturity.

In my interviews I found that intimate and meaningful relationships are a highly valued commodity in their lives, but since they are no longer in the business of having or raising children and are learning to enjoy their independence, marriage does not seem to be an attraction. Ninety-eight percent said they wanted independence, financial security, intimacy, relationships, romance, laughter, sharing, and the ability to pursue their interests. Marriage was not mentioned as a desirable option.

There is no denying that there are tremendous benefits to having a man in your life. Intimacy, companionship and conversation are all things a man offers a woman that we happily accept and return. Many have come to the realization that they can obtain these moments from their selected companions without having to marry them. The value of love in our lives is a much-proven benefit. Love of a mate, children, family, friends, and our pets—it all matters. Personally, my life has been a bit more interesting, challenging, and fun when a man of worth has walked into it. I am grateful to those few men I have known in my life who have loved me, and I them. We learned much from each other. I have learned one indisputable fact, and that is that many of us, as mature women, have the right to enjoy love and share our lives with a special man without having to marry him. It has become a standard option, a choice. Times have changed.

As for those women who remain married and find themselves happy in their choices, I applaud them. We should equally embrace those who find themselves at the end of their marriages and starting over. Some by choice, others by force, whatever the reason, they are quickly discovering the struggles and benefits of life without a husband.

MARRIAGE HAD ITS MOMENT

There is a time in our life when marriage is a wonderful way to be with one's true love. This generally occurs when we are young, starting out, creating families, and building careers. If it works, it is amazing. If it doesn't, it is a life sadly lived.

No one marries with the thought she may become irreparably unhappy and see her relationship end in divorce, but statistics tell us that it is a 50/50 chance at best. It is easier to take that chance when you are in your twenties, thirties, and even forties. However, having reached a certain age, we discover that our priorities have changed along with us, and that marriage is no longer the only option, and often, may not be the best choice.

It is my philosophy that everyone should be married at least once. Marriage teaches us so many things. We learn to love, share, compromise, and, in most cases, how to be mothers. Could we have learned all of these things without the benefit of marriage? Undoubtedly. But the truth is, when we are in our younger years, we hold love as a forever ideal. We have not yet experienced the realities called marriage, and it is wonderful that we give it our very best shot. As well-seasoned women, we take the knowledge we garnered in our marriage(s) to help us in making the decision to choose to remain single.

As women over 50, we realize that it is clearly our choice of lifestyle that should be well thought out and evenly measured for its value. A choice made in a moment's time will affect our entire lives. We have more to lose in making rash or uninformed decisions. Unlike our younger sisters, we no longer have 50 healthy, productive years ahead of us. For the woman over 50, being a couple is an attractive option. Less can be said for being a married couple.

DEVOTION AND DECEPTION

An important observation about marriage that every once-married woman has made is that it often begins with a mountain of untruths. The deception for men and women is unintentional, but we now know the truths about love, life, and the pursuit of happiness. For example, when we hear the words, love, honor and obey, in sickness and in health, for richer or poorer, until death do you part, we know it's a bit of a crock. Of course, we entered with the best of intentions, but as my grandfather would say, "The road to hell is paved with good intentions." Experience has taught us that these vows are somewhat unreasonable, although sweet in sentiment.

There are many other untruths we told our partner, as well as ourselves. We need to give ourselves credit for trying, for daring to love the best we knew how in that moment of time, but we are no longer those young, naive women.

Our years and our tears have taught us well. Women over 50 are smart. Our lives and our loves will be about reality. We are becoming more interested in what works rather than what is expected of us. We have already followed the rules set forth by society, our parents, and our peers. Been there, done that. We will make our own rules this time around and we will be better for it.

TAMMY-ISM: *Look, there are definite things that I do not like about being an un-couple. No matter how empowered I feel when I go to a movie alone, I still have a twinge of loser-itis that accompanies my independence. Same thing goes for eating out alone. I'm not a huge fan of being a* *party of one at a restaurant. Seriously, why should I continue to attempt to be good at something that I don't like doing and is not required? I say forget it. I don't give a rat's butt if society says that I'm well-adjusted if I am able to eat alone at a restaurant and be completely comfortable. I'm <u>not</u> completely comfortable, and I <u>am</u> well-adjusted!*

And by the way, there were plenty of things I didn't like about being a couple. Some of my loneliest moments occurred during my marriage, and often when my husband was in the same room. But, it was better than being single, right? Not by a long shot!

Memory is a good thing. It helps to balance out the truth of life. Selective memory can be convenient, but it will never produce truth. There are good and bad things about being married and about being un-married. Few of us ever really weigh them against each other until we are either at the point where the misery slaps us in the face or our spouse does it for us.

Taking stock and measuring what is so hot about being married or what is so hot about being single is a very cleansing act. It can also be shocking. I remember reasoning with myself for years before I made the move to be single. Did I really want to be all alone, single, starting over at 40 years of age? Each time I asked myself that question my age had increased. What is scarier than starting over at 40? The answer would be starting over at 46 or 50 or 60 years of age. Fear of being an un-couple was the biggest and the least of my worries. Get over it. Life gets better when you live happy.

THE UPSIDE OF SINGLEDOM

*A woman's rule of thumb: If it has tires
or testicles, you're going to have trouble with it.*

- Women's restroom, Dick's Last Resort, Dallas TX

I'm really not sure which has given me more trouble: tires or testicles. What I like about tires is, if they give me grief, I can change or rotate or repair them. Problems in the testicle department represent a commitment of time, patience, energy, blah, blah, blah. In short (no pun intended) the return must be worth the investment. Sometimes it is, and sometimes it just isn't. That's okay because there are many advantages to being testicle-less—I mean, single.

It's no longer our biological clock that is loudly ticking; it is our life's clock we hear in the echoes of our minds. If you are over 50 and newly single, you are probably more aware of the time you have left and experiencing some fear issues and sizeable doubts for what the future may hold. You are on your own, dependent on only yourself. You have your future to consider, and things may seem a little uncertain at present. The ground you have been standing on for years has been shaken, and everything is different now. Put your fear away, my friend; being single at this time in your life is a good thing.

You are not alone. Single America represents 42% of the workforce, 40% of homebuyers, 35% of voters, and we are members of one of the most potent consumer groups in America (Unmarried America 2005). The number of women passing through middle age is so vast a group—there are roughly 43 million American women ages 40 to 60—that it guarantees some rules will be rewritten and boundaries moved (Gibbs 2005).

Unlike the generations before us, we are creating a new definition for midlife. Whether through divorce, death of a spouse or parent, children leaving the nest, or menopause, women must be resilient beyond their expectations. After an initial period of reflection and healing, we strike out to pursue a passion lost, a career not yet achieved, a goal never reached. We assess our lives in hard-hitting ways to see where we are headed and where we want to be in 10 or 20 years. Then we act. If you're not there yet, you will be.

You are no longer married for good reason, and we must all play the cards we have been dealt. It is comforting to know there are a lot of up sides to being single past 50. As mature women, our advantages are many, and it's about time we recognized them. It's time for us to dream and have goals for ourselves. Seriously, let's get on with it.

In a *TIME Magazine* article (Gibbs 2005) which addressed the growing number of middle-aged women embracing life's changes, psychoanalyst Carl Jung is cited as stating that women tend to put their dreams on a shelf during the child-rearing years, becoming bolder and more able to dream as they get older. Gibbs' own research tends to support Jung's conclusions. Thirty-six percent of women between 50 and 64 reported that they had fulfilled a dream, compared with 24% of younger women and 28% of their male peers. We are able to take more risks as we become less concerned with what those around us will think. We quickly begin to realize that our lives, to date governed by our families' needs, now belong only to us. There is a lot of excitement in that realization.

You must also recognize that we are a hell of a lot smarter about life than when we were younger. We are far more knowledgeable about people, business, and how the world operates. It would be difficult to put something over on a 50-year-old woman, but a cinch to do so to a 20- year-old version of ourselves. We have firsthand knowledge of how things work, what makes them work, and how to make things happen for ourselves.

It is well documented and has been the subject of numerous articles of prominent news magazines that women over 50 are not accepting midlife and being single as some kind of death sentence. Rather, they are embracing the notion of being free and making some astonishing leaps.

This time in your life is the time to think about YOU. When was the last time you did that? To be a bit selfish and indulgent with your wants and needs, that is the name of this new game. Wives and mothers are excellent at putting themselves last on the list. We often don't even notice how much we give up in doing so. In essence, we give away a piece of ourselves. It is time to reclaim what it is you want for your life.

SHOW ME THE MONEY

Money is often a little more available at this stage of our life. We are no longer spending thousands a year on new shoes, party dresses, and the latest styles for our kids. Gone are the days when the price of soccer camp was more important than the visit back home you wanted to take. Spend on yourself. You can start purchasing some new clothes for yourself that are of this decade's style and get rid of those items in your closet that are over five years old. Sexy clothing is no longer forbidden. You no longer have to worry what your child's friends will say about mom when they come over to hang out. Express yourself and your own sense of style.

Did you know that according to SmartMoney magazine, 40% of women and 36% of men have lied to their spouses about a purchase? When you are single, you are accountable only to yourself. When you are married, you are tied to your husband's spending and saving habits, as well as his debt. If the marriage does not make it to forever, it can have an awesomely negative effect on your financial situation. Researchers at Ohio State University's Center for Human Resource Research have found that during a divorce, men and women generally lose three-fourths of their personal net worth. Yikes!

Mobility is a huge plus. If you get a call from a friend who wants to meet up for coffee, dinner or a movie, you are free to go! There is no one to check with. No approval needed. Traveling, socializing, having more time to do the things you want to do will become part of your everyday life. While married couples dominate the travel market with 62% of all trips taken, singles hold the line for far more interesting trips. Being footloose and fancy free, we are not bound to the traditional family vacations, rather we are opting for more active and exotic activities and locations.

You finally have the time to take up those hobbies you previously had so little energy for. I spoke with a woman who was divorced after 31 years of marriage, and she was so happy to finally have the time to join a women's travel club and learn how to make quilts. Through those two avenues, she has forged some wonderful friendships and finds her life richer and happier. Whatever your interests—whether it's books, dog shows, traveling, motorcycles, snorkeling—you've got the time. Do it!

TIME TO ACHIEVE

The idea of starting our own businesses has proven to be a viable and exciting option for the single, mature woman. Many of us need to work in order to pay the bills. When we do a cost analysis of working at a job we don't enjoy versus taking a leap of faith and giving ourselves a new opportunity, more and more of us are willing to jump. Part of the joy is the control factor, part is the excitement, and part is doing something new on our own. As single, mature women, we are more in touch with our capabilities, and given time, we find our creativity.

Housework? You have a lot less of it. And that equals free time, lots of it, for reading, movies, traveling, friendships, or just hanging with the cat.

Alone time is one of the most precious gifts that unmarried women have. It will give you the chance to discover who you are, who you want to be, and how you want to live the rest of your life. If you need to be sad, you cry. If you are afraid, you contemplate and think to solve. If you're happy, you relish. Our alone time helps us work through whatever we are facing and recharge our energies for the tasks that lay ahead.

BEAUTY WITHOUT THE PRICE

Would you believe me if I told you that single women generally have better and healthier bodies? A recent Cornell University study found that women generally gain five to eight pounds in the first few years of marriage and unhappily married women gain an average of 54 pounds in the first 10 years (Yanek 2007). Hello? Did everyone hear that?

Women over 50 represent large numbers of gym memberships. It's not that we have become obese and unsightly, but more often, that we finally have the time to dedicate to ourselves. We experience better health, new friendships, and new interests. Clare, one woman I interviewed, is a 50-year-old woman who was married for 27 years and had three kids. She explained to me that she always wanted to have time to join a gym, but with carpools, hockey games, Girl Scout meetings, PTA events, her husband's needs, and the housekeeping, it was simply impossible. Almost every married woman knows about this lack of time; sad, but true. Today, however, this is no longer the case for Clare.

Health is another advantage of being single. When you go to the grocery store, what you find in your basket are the things you like, not what the kids or your husband want. Single women tend to eat smarter. Their stress levels also are notably lower. As single women, we often lead healthier lives because we are in charge of ourselves and actually have the time and the resources to do what we need to do, and more importantly, what we want to do.

Women are excellent at networking and supporting each other. At least 22 studies (Unmarried America 2005) have shown that having social support decreases the heart racing, blood-pressure-boosting responses that humans and other social animals experience when stressed. Researchers at Ohio State University and Carnegie Mellon University have shown that people who report strong social supports have more robust immune systems and are less likely to succumb to infectious disease.

FRIENDSHIPS THAT BIND

Throughout our culture, women have banded together for protection, friendship, and mutual support. They communicate with each other on levels that men usually do not. They share, encourage, and listen. The single, mature woman has more time and energy to strengthen those friendships she has and to develop new ones. Friendships profoundly affect your health.

According to Dr. James J. Lynch, a Maryland-based author and psychologist, loneliness is one of the principal causes of premature death in this country. Men and women who report loneliness die earlier, get sick more often, and weather transitions with greater physical wear and tear than those who say they have a support network. Unfortunately, because men often rely heavily on their wives to assist them in warding off the corrosive health effects of age and loneliness, they do not usually fare as well once they are divorced (Unmarried America 2005).

For women, evidence shows that in times of stress, a male partner can make things worse. In a study published in the journal *Psychosomatic Medicine* in 1995, German researchers found that when subjects were given a stressful task, men who were joined by their female partners showed much lower stress levels than those who had no support. Women, however, when joined by their male partners, found that their stress hormones surged. This is not news to any married woman (Unmarried America 2005).

Married men live longer and healthier lives than do bachelors or widowers (Unmarried America 2005). It doesn't take a nuclear scientist to see why. Wives take care of their husbands. They are the driving force to get them to the doctor for check-ups: they watch their husbands' diets and cholesterol levels. They are, in short, the angel on a husband's shoulder. As a general rule, husbands do not reciprocate this care to their wives.

When you are married, you are often called upon to make compromises; not that learning to compromise is a bad thing. It is essential to any successful relationship, whether it be personal or business. But a lifetime of compromises can certainly take its toll. It would not be an unfair statement to say that women often do the majority of compromising in marriage. Compromise of career, worldly possessions, time with peers, and time for self is only the tip of the iceberg. It is important to note that exceptions to this rule of thumb do indeed exist, but they are not the norm.

RESTED, RELAXED AND REFRESHED

Sleeping alone IS all it's cracked up to be. The National Sleep Foundation has reported that your bedmate can cause you to lose an average of 49 minutes of sleep a night. Other studies support the fact that singles get more rest, often 7 to 8 hours a night. The added rest allows your immune system to recharge itself and enhances your moods, concentration and memory (Yanek 2007).

The single life provides you with a peaceful world requiring little or no compromise. It's wonderful. There is no one telling you to change the channel, stop reading and turn the light off, cook something a certain way, stop leaving the newspaper on the table—the list is endless. It's your home, and everything in it is run your way. Wonderfully, cereal for dinner is okay, staying in your pajamas on a rainy Saturday afternoon just reading and napping is undebatable; whether the animals will be allowed to sleep on the bed or not is not up for negotiation. There is a lot to be said for that, and if you are anything like me, you never realized how peaceful and calm your world could be.

And then there is dating. Meeting new people, getting out and about, going to movies, dinners, the theater, Sunday picnics, sharing intimate conversation and emotions. Research (AARP 2003) tells us that the older a person gets, the more he or she becomes a practical dater, as opposed to being emotionally driven.

According to the vice-president of romance at Match. com, single Americans over 55 are the group least likely to believe their romantic lives are controlled by destiny, or that they only have one soul mate. They bring realistic expectations to the table and are found to be more flexible and open-minded about finding someone. Singles in their fifties often have greater wisdom and more grace in dealing with people, qualities that make new friendships and potential romances far more likely and enjoyable.

And let's talk about sex. It has been documented that married couples have more sex, BUT singles have better sex. A recent study in the British Medical Journal support the findings that people who are single are having better sex because it's new and exciting. It is reported that sex is hotter during the first two years of a relationship. Long-term lovers have to work harder at keeping it frisky, new, and interesting. Mature women are at a high advantage in that they know what they want and they are usually good at articulating it. Ask and you will receive is the general consensus.

HAPPY, NOT SAD

It's funny how the single woman is often portrayed as being lonely and sad, when the opposite has been proven. A recent report by the World Health Organization indicated that women who are married, especially if they have children, have a higher rate of depression than single women. It is also a fact that single women generally have fewer mental health issues than their married counterparts (Yanek 2007). The life of the single woman often lends itself to the ability to invest itself in a healthy way. The married woman rarely enjoys this opportunity.

These are just a few of the many advantages of being single over 50. You will discover some of your own when you allow yourself to live for you.

TAMMY-ISM: *Being single is absolutely fabulous! Yeah, right. Not so much at first. At first it stunk, mostly because I stunk at being single. No one, not a friend, not a relative, not a divorce recovery expert, no one ever mentioned that being single and being good at it entailed a truckload of effort. You heard it here.*

Once I got past all the negative bull that littered my day to day, it was much easier to have a pleasant life. By the way, it was mostly me that littered my life with all that negative bull. Oh, at the time, I blamed my ex-husband completely. He caused so many of my problems and hardships. A

few months into the muck, I got tired of myself—
my whining, my crying, and my bitching. It
occurred to me (and none too soon) that whoever
coined the phrase, "it's not what happens, its how
you deal with it", was a bloody genius!

Being single really is fabulous. Now, since I put
in the effort. I gave myself time. I made myself
accountable. The upsides still surprise me. I
honestly cannot imagine my life being any better,
really. Anything worth having is worth working
for, and anything great is going to be work.

PAST VS. PRESENT

There are dreams of love, life, and adventure in all of us. But we are also sadly filled with reasons why we shouldn't try. These reasons seem to protect us, but in truth they imprison us. They hold life at a distance. Life will be over sooner than we think. If we have bikes to ride and people to love, now is the time.

- ELISABETH KUBLER-ROSS

Our past is history, our future a mystery. When we were younger, life seemed not to have an expiration date. The rules were different, and the status quo seemed to offer lower expectations. We know so much more today than we did years ago. That goes for pretty much every field: medicine, law, aviation, psychology, family values, women's issues, and political correctness.

Why, then, would we think for a moment that the status of the single woman would stay the same? It is now very common for women to be in the workplace. It is also mainstream for women to be single, unattached mothers. In contrast to our life styles of 20 or 30 years ago, these situations are part of the natural order of things in our world today.

One thing hasn't changed: the often male-run industry that capitalizes on women's needs, desires, and fears. There is much money to be made here. From the financial point of view, wouldn't you love to be profiting from the millions of dollars made by one of the Internet dating sites? Hundreds of agencies make millions of dollars feeding off the frenzy created by the theory that we must couple up in order to be happy.

Industries such as these are huge moneymakers, and the end does not appear to be in sight. It is sad that many of these agencies promote their services by encouraging fear in women. They reinforce the notion that the only way you will be truly happy is to find your soul mate. It's good for business, but the message is way off base. Unfortunately, many women buy into this propagated nonsense.

Businesses are realizing that there is a market out there that is not being tapped. Unmarried Americans account for over 1.6 trillion dollars spent every year on product purchases (Unmarried America 2005). Women make the majority of these purchasing decisions. Answering to the call of good business, some are jumping on the bandwagon.

De Beers, one of the world's top diamond producers, launched an ad campaign directed towards the mature, single woman. Smart! Their slogans: "Your left hand is your heart. Your right hand is your voice." and "Your left hand says 'we.' Your right hand says 'me.'" These marketing ads simply validate the fact that the woman over 50 knows what she wants and is willing to purchase it herself rather than wait to be gifted.

Cruise lines are now tailoring voyages towards the single, mature woman. Bulk food stores have begun stocking items packaged in single servings. Health clubs have modified their packages to include the single woman and her close friends or children.

Single past 50 is more the norm than the exception. Higher divorce rates, longer life spans, and a greater tendency to never marry are factors responsible for churning out more single American women than at any other time in our country's history. Of the 97 million Americans who are 45 or older, almost 40% (or 36.2 million) are on the loose, according to the U.S. Census Bureau (2001). It has begun. We have arrived. The only problem is…many of us have not yet realized it.

Do you recall a long-ago television program called *Queen for a Day*? This very successful program of the fifties featured three women of different walks of life and focused on their strife and poverty. Basically, the one with the most tragic story, the most tears, would win the washer and dryer or new refrigerator. The audience would vote, and the decision was measured on a primitive needle meter activated by audience applause. I can pretty much guarantee you that a woman did not conceive this concept of entertainment, nor did a woman profit from it. It was, and is, a man's world. While the day of blatantly exploiting women may appear to have reached its pinnacle, it is perhaps really only the method of exploitation that has changed.

It is important for us to remember that we are the generation that grew up watching television shows like *Donna Reed, Leave it to Beaver,* and of course, *Father Knows Best.* For many, these shows exemplified the ideal of a good wife and mother.

I always pictured myself with a pretty little apron, a string of pearls around my neck and a husband who brought home the bacon while I stayed home and cleaned house, cooked fabulous meals, and raised the kids (each of whom would not have any problems that couldn't be solved in a half-hour's time). It's important to remember those images that influenced us when we were children. They may explain some of our reluctance to ride the current wave of freedom due us. No excuses. Letting go of old standards is essential for our happiness and success.

TAMMY-ISM: *I will admit that one of my biggest fears is having regrets. To date I have three very large and looming regrets that consume more of my present-day thought than they should. The really lousy thing about* *those things we regret is that it's done. It's over. You cannot change it; you cannot will it to be different. I really believe that our regrets impact who we are and who we aren't.*

My upbringing was very modest, to say the least. The fanciest store I ever shopped at was Newberry's. I went to my first department store when I was 20. I was always taught to know my place and respect my station in life. The importance of being a lady, a wife, and a mother is something that was embedded daily. No other options existed. Nor were they ever offered. This mind-set was bestowed on me by the very person I loved and admired most, my mom; and questioning its logic never occurred to me until years later. Mom tried her best with what she knew. What she knew was her past upbringing, past values, and past limitations. It defined her. It did not, in the end, define me.

Our past can easily explain our present and influence our future. I believe with my whole heart that I need to be vigilant so as not to slump into past tendencies toward low expectations and accepting self-imposed limitations. Way easier said than done! I don't always succeed. But my advice to you is to keep one eye on the future and one eye on your past. Knowing one will help achieve what you want for the other. Go for it with all your might.

OUR GREATEST FEARS

Feel the fear, and do it anyway.

- Susan Jeffers

I seem to collect fears like a lint roller collects lint. There are few emotions more powerful than fear. Woman past the age of 50 know it all too well. If allowed to live and grow, fear will dictate, dominate, and destroy.

We all have our demons: they are as much a part of us as our fingerprints. Few people can understand what haunts another human being. To them, a particular fear might seem trivial or easily managed. It is only the living of our lives that can explain them. If a particular fear daunts you, then that same fear is capable of crippling your spirit.

As women, we are susceptible to fear. It's how we were brought up. Our parent(s) often told us that we were unable to accomplish certain tasks merely because of our gender. I remember my mother telling me to marry a nice boy who would take care of me because going to college would be too difficult and too expensive.

I followed my mother's advice, as many daughters do. I'm sure she meant well, but the results were disastrous because the assumption was untrue. I believe this advice was fear based and passed on to me because this was the way my mother was raised to think.

It was a generational act, one of trying to protect and guide, but in reality, her advice only assured me that I needed a husband to succeed and be happy. It took me years to figure it out. I believe there are thousands of women out there in a similar circumstance. If you can't trust your mom or dad, who can you believe? Good question. The answer, of course, is you.

Hindsight is twenty/twenty, but at the time, we all would have been hard-pressed to believe our parents didn't know what they were talking about. Make no mistake; we know the advice given to us by them was offered out of care and love. There is no blame to be placed here, just recognition that we were misinformed. Recognize, also, that we are capable of so much more and deserving of all good things. It is, however, a stumbling block most women will need to overcome. It is not an easy task, but if we are to spread our wings and fly high, overcoming old stigmas and expectations are part of the deal.

The real problem with our fears, of course, is that they come from within us. Those little voices in our heads that give us 30 reasons why we can't or shouldn't do those things that are our heart's desire. They are the "what ifs" that stop us cold every time. They are us at our weakest. Let's be honest, ladies, there isn't anyone we listen to more during the course of a day than ourselves.

It is my opinion that the outline below represents a valuable measure of our emotions and their ability to help or hinder us along the way.

The most destructive habit . . . . Worry

The worst thing to be without . . . . .Hope

The most worthless emotion. . . . . .Self-pity

The greatest loss . . . . Self-respect

The two most powerful words . . . . I can

The greatest problem to overcome . . . . Fear

My research confirmed what I already knew in my gut: the woman over 50 has more fears than a dog has fleas. Let's look at the top 10 fears identified in my survey. Top fears experienced by single women over 50 are:

Poverty

Loneliness/living alone

Not being loved

Being incapable/ill or injured

Growing old/dying alone

Being a burden to their children

Failing

Fear of dating

Rejection

Reentering the workforce

If you think you have an original fear, you don't.

If you think you are alone in your fears, you're not.

If you think your fears can take you down, you're right.

If you think you can overcome your fears, you will.

In interviewing single women over 50, I found interesting the commonalities that many of us share— there were some surprises. Let me share some of their wisdom with you, and see if you recognize yourself.

JEAN

I was married for 31 years, not terribly unhappy ones, but not happy, either. If it were not for my fears, I probably would have left long before I did. It sounds silly now, but the truth is, I had never lived or slept alone in my life. I just didn't know how, and the idea petrified me. Who would have known that the day my husband moved out, I slept that night like a baby and have ever since. As for living alone, well, let's just say that I absolutely love it!

SHARON

Married for 19 years, with three kids, you would think I would be fearless. Finances were my big fear. Not being able to pay the bills, make the money, do taxes, or even balance my checkbook. In all the years of marriage, I did none of the above. The fear of taking on those financial responsibilities and failing miserably kept me in a relationship that was unhappy, unrewarding and stifling. I still can't balance my checkbook very well, but I am having no problems bringing home the bacon and paying the bills. Oh, and I hired an accountant to do the taxes.

LIZZIE

I married my college sweetheart. We were together for 35 years. I was happy to make sacrifices to help my husband get ahead. It was, after all, for the greater good. It didn't take long for me to realize that he was not willing to do the same for me. There were a lot of problems from the beginning. But the children came along and life went on. I know now that what really kept me in place was my one huge overbearing fear: the fear that no one else would ever love me. What if he was the only opportunity I would ever have? In the end, I would discover that it wasn't about someone else loving me: it was about me loving myself enough. Who knew?

PAMELLA

The thought of growing old alone, of maybe becoming sick or poor, kept me in a miserable marriage for 26 years. Once I got past that disabling fear, I haven't looked back. I love my life. I now run my own catering business and honestly am looking forward to my older years...on my own!

Fear is the voice in your head constantly speaking to you, giving you bad pieces of information, reinforcing what is not true. It is often disguised as logic. It is the enemy. Fear is the one thing that will stand between you and the life you could—you should—lead. If you allow it to live in you, it will take you down every time.

It's important to acknowledge that there are two kinds of fear: good fear, and bad fear. The good fear is the kind that will save you, and keep you safe and alive. It will keep you from going to the very edge of a cliff or will stop you from walking down that alley in the dark of night. Women use it every day. We try to teach it to our kids. While some would say it is just instinct, it is still unmitigated fear, and its presence in us will help keep us from going down unsafe paths.

There is a way to combat the bad fear, and it may surprise you in its simplicity. The answer lies within you. Practice talking to yourself as you would when encouraging your best friend or your child to accomplish a given goal. Each and every time you give yourself reasons why you cannot do something, make it a task to write down five things that would be better in your life if you were to try and succeed at the goal. Take it further. Write down 10 reasons how you could accomplish the task. When you start to worry that you're being selfish or silly, verbally stop yourself right then and there. You would not listen to negative verbiage from your daughter or son in putting themselves down, and you should NOT put up with it from yourself.

If you're waiting for the fear to leave, stop waiting. I'm not sure it ever does. I'm also not sure we should want it to. I think it's always lingering inside. Hopefully, we learn to manage it, control it, and not let it get the best of us. We must put one foot in front of the other and give it our best shot.

Accomplishments and growth only come with the trying. Julia Soul said, "If you are never scared, embarrassed, or hurt, it means you never take chances." We cannot, must not, let fear keep us from taking chances.

Fear speaks to all of us. It is part of our every day. There are still times I am compelled to keep a light on. I honestly could not explain why. For those of us who overanalyze, fear is an unwelcome guest that stays for the duration. It's woven into the fabric of our mind-set. I am working on changing my mind-set. Because I know I can.

TAMMY-ISM: *I'm going to tell you right now that I'm a big ball of fears. A big ball! It's okay, though, because I think I have learned how to keep a handle on my fears and make them work for me (well, most of the time.) I don't think any of us ever rids ourselves of our fears. Maybe the best we can hope for is recognizing them for what they are, because conquering fear takes more than courage. It takes knowing what it is you're up against.*

These days even with all that I've learned, fear still grabs me, but seldom will it stop me. When I did my first public speaking engagement so many years ago it seems like another life, I remember pure fear in my gut. I peeked behind the curtain before I went out on stage and saw over a hundred people. I froze. Suddenly I was sick to my stomach and ran over to the trashcan and vomited, and then, vomited some more. After a few minutes I could hear my intro. I honestly don't remember walking on to the stage, but I did. Neither do I remember my first five minutes up there—they must have been terrible. I do remember the standing ovation I received after my presentation, and I have not let fear stop me since that day.

LONELINESS

To dare to live alone is the rarest courage;
for there are many who would rather
meet their bitterest enemy in the field,
than their own hearts in the closet.

- CHARLES CALEB COLTON

To be alone, to live alone, is a brave thing. Women are brave: perhaps that is why we are twice as likely to live alone than men. We have been told that happiness is a state of mind, a state of being. Many of us equate being single with being alone, lonely, and sad. In the beginning stages of being alone, this may be the case, but only because we are healing our wounds with solitude, thought, and time. It is purposeful alone time.

Not too long ago, my daughter asked me, "What's so great about being single?" Doesn't everyone want to love and be loved? The answer is as simple as it is true: being single does not equate with being alone, not if you are doing it correctly.

Single people love and are loved by friends, family and the opposite sex. Have we forgotten the concept of the boyfriends and best girlfriends? Still, loneliness often attacks us when we find ourselves single again. To a degree, self-confinement can be a good thing; to be lonely is not.

Many of us confuse loneliness with actually being alone. They couldn't be more polar. When we spend healthy time alone, it is often by our own choice and for our own benefit. Snuggling on the couch with some hot tea and reading a good book, walking and listening to your favorite music, gardening, going to the gym, even shopping alone can be a most refreshing and rejuvenating time. Loneliness is a different matter entirely.

When we lose something, we are left with a longing and a loneliness. A child goes to college, a spouse dies, a marriage ends, a best friend moves to another state. All result in a loss and in the loneliness of missing the happiness that once was. Without exception, we must face it, accept it, and take actions to ensure that it does not consume us, because left to fester, it can.

We begin by admitting that we are lonely. It is always easier to resolve a problem once it is acknowledged. Alcoholics Anonymous was built on the foundation of this fact. Once a problem is acknowledged, you are then able to take the necessary steps to remedy it.

Physical contact is an amazing tool in fighting loneliness. People who own pets benefit from a healthier immune system and a happier and longer life. Why? Studies conclude it is because they experience the act of touching, holding, petting, loving and being loved. Pets offer what people most often cannot: unconditional love and unquestioning loyalty. They are that beating heart, that warm breath which assures you that you are not alone. We need them as much as they need us, and at different intervals of our lives, we sometimes need them more.

Pet owners usually get out and walk their dogs, play with their cats, indulge them with various toys, balls, and catnip. In return our pets make us laugh and feel loved. They radiate warmth and acceptance. It is a win-win relationship, and I wholeheartedly recommend it.

I had an aunt who lived alone all of her life. She isolated herself from the world and confined her existence to her home and a couple of family members. She spoke little English, and never integrated into mainstream society. She was self-sufficient in her self-built world and appeared to be very happy in her lifestyle choice. I visited her monthly and what meant most to her were my hugs—the sharing of human contact. She would embrace me, long and hard, and sometimes I would see her eyes well up. Just the act of touching each other for a brief moment made her feel less lonely. The power of touch is the power of caring.

Conversation, the sharing of emotions, is another strong defeater of loneliness. To be able to talk and share ourselves with each other brings us closer to people who care enough to listen. We then can experience listening, and often what we discover is understanding and support. The inability or unwillingness to share emotions and thoughts and to listen have been the downfall of many a relationship.

As women we have a gift, an innate ability, to pour out with passionate abandon what is hurting us and what we fear. We are also very willing to listen to the other person with the same passionate concern. When we allow ourselves to share, to communicate our emotions, we cut the strings that bind us to loneliness.

TAMMY-ISM: *Doesn't everyone alive know what it's like to be lonely? Of course they do, we all do. Loneliness is part of living. We can't always be up and happy and surrounded by hoards of people who love us. I think the real problem is that loneliness is a sneaky son-of-a-bitch. Before you know it, wham! It smacks you in the face. I speak from experience. I invited it. No, I welcomed it. There was something almost comforting to my loneliness. I made sure there was no one there to reprimand me, no one to report to, no one to nag me, and no one to love me. It seemed so easy, and it was. I discovered that the problem was, loneliness had a price tag: happiness. I chose not to pay it. Being social takes a little effort. So what? It's like rolling a snowball: the beginning effort is work, but it gets easier and bigger and better as you progress. Make it happen; you have done harder things in your life.*

OUR GREATEST GIFTS

Women who aspire to be as good as men,
lack ambition.

- ANONYMOUS

I love this quote. I wish I knew who "anonymous" was so I could kiss them on the lips.

The funny thing about our gifts is that we rarely recognize them. It's hard to appreciate something if you don't know it's there. Our abilities are our strengths, and our strengths are our gifts.

OTHER WOMEN

There is an amazing ability women have: the ability to tap into the undivided attention and expertise of other women. Some may label it the gift of gab. That would be an understatement. The presence in our lives of friends, co-workers, daughters, mothers, and sisters is an undeniable strength. Because women have the ability to communicate with each other so well in a very brief amount of time exactly what is happening in their mind and heart, they can, and usually do, receive immediate, caring feedback.

We women will cut to the chase and tell it like it is. It doesn't matter if the other woman is a co-worker who has only known us for a week. If we have a problem and share it, chances are pretty good she is right there trying to help us work it out. We are natural marketers of our fears and problems, and our instinct to share them with other women is a salvaging one. It is really astonishing how we can band together for each other, no matter the length or brevity of our relationship.

When a woman finds the key to fulfilling her own midlife needs, she is more than anxious to help others do the same. It is this kindred spirit that exists among us, and it is an amazing skill to possess and share.

OUR SKILLS

We all have within us certain skills. Some have the ability to cook up a storm, some to work a crossword puzzle in record time. Others can manage finances with the greatest of ease. Our job is to tap into what we do best and capitalize on it. This is easier said than done, but doing it can make the difference between a life happily led and one of mediocrity. Many a career has been launched by a mature woman who found herself suddenly self-dependent.

Who do you think you are? Or, more importantly, who do you want to be? This is the question you must ask yourself, and in time, give yourself a well-thought-out answer. Have you always wanted to be a public speaker, a teacher, a real estate mogul, or an artist? There is an old saying: Follow your heart, and the money will follow.

While the money sometimes takes a bit of time to find you, it will. Happiness, however, is an immediate guarantee. When you are happy doing something, you will do it with all your heart, you will spend a lot of time on it, and you will produce. Let's be honest, happiness is extremely vital, but so is money.

All mature women know that money is about freedom— the freedom to be independent, afford health care, to be able to help your kids financially, and to provide for yourself without worry. Women don't equate money with a big house and an expensive, fancy car. They equate it with their ability to live a free and fulfilling life.

PAMELLA

Pretty much all my adult life I enjoyed cooking. When I was tense, angry or nervous, I would cook. I cooked for all my friends' parties and always received rave reviews. With no college degree to fall back on, I was panicky after my divorce as to how I would earn a living. It was my girlfriends who helped me to understand that I had an obvious talent. Their encouragement prodded me. When I lacked confidence, it seemed as though I borrowed it from them. My low self-esteem had me thinking of working as a cook in a local restaurant. My friends encouraged me to be brave and have confidence in myself. They dared me to dream, and I did. I started a small catering business with a friend who joined me just to help. The two of us bungled our way through making flyers, creating a business logo and a marketing plan. It took surprising little time to get bookings. My ability to cook and manage a small business is putting my son through college, paying my bills, and allowing me to put a little away each month. I would never have found this independence and daily joy of going to work had I stayed married or listened to my fears. Sometimes good things really do come from bad experiences.

LIZZIE

I have always had a love of the outdoors: camping, hiking, breaking new ground. I dealt with the hardships in my marriage by going out and being alone in the great outdoors. When the divorce was final, I was clueless about finding work. It had been years since I was part of the workforce, and I knew I was ill equipped. A friend told me I should start some kind of business that involved my love for the outdoors. After laughing it off, a group of friends met one night for drinks, and before the evening was over, we had devised a plan. I now operate a successful guide business for children and adults. I work with the school districts and am employed as an independent contractor to take groups out into the wilderness to learn and explore. I love getting up in the morning and going to work.

GAYLE

I was a corporate worker all during my married years. I ran an office with over 40 employees, as well as taking care of a household with two kids, two dogs, a cat, and, of course, a husband. I hated the rat race, the pressures, the deadlines, but I spent years in college for the degree, and it was all I knew how to do. When my divorce was final, I did some real soul-searching. With the help of my daughter and sister, I found a new path. I am the proud owner of a doggie day care. It still makes me laugh that I am making close to the same amount of money as before, have twice as much free time and half the stress. I work with dogs all day and I love it. I enjoy my life so much more these days, and am looking to possibly expand with franchises. Escaping the fast track, I live a fuller life thanks to the wonderful women who saw in me something I never imagined...guts.

OUR HOPEFUL SPIRITS

Researchers (Gibbs 2005) have found that the most profound difference in attitude between men and women at middle age is that women are twice as likely to be hopeful about the future. Hopefulness is something women have embedded in their spirit. We have been trained, subdued, and often beaten down, but the spirit still lives. It is that ability to remain hopeful that often leads us toward success.

A good friend of mine who is a physiologist once told me a story that he believed depicted the difference between men and women. He pictured a man and a woman, dirt poor, living in a shack near a railroad track. With little money and even scarcer hope of acquiring any, the man dealt with his depression by getting drunk. The woman went out and found a discarded pop bottle, put a little water in it, and picked some wildflowers to place on their table. She found ways to make things appear better, even if she couldn't make things better. While an absolute generalization, there is much truth to be found in this analogy.

It is our spirit to hope, to dream, to think, and, in the end, to try that sets us apart. You have this spirit in you: even if you are unaware of it. Your lack of awareness doesn't negate its existence. Your job: find your spirit of hope and adventure. Embrace it, and you will be guided down the road to happiness.

OUR CHILDREN

I firmly believe, for those of us who have grown children, we can find in them a wealth of help and information. They have known us all their lives, and if we have done our jobs well, they will be there for us.

The great thing about our kids is their honesty. They pull no punches. They don't have to worry about hurting our feelings because they know we are guaranteed to love them no matter what. I can always count on my daughter to tell me the truth about my wardrobe selection, my hairstyle, and my makeup. She is equally honest with me about my career goals, and sometimes, about the lack of them.

The mistake many women make is to assume they are the final word of wisdom. They are, after all, much older and wiser than their kids. What we often fail to see is the value their opinions bring. They know us for who we really are, not just how we present ourselves to the world. They know our strengths as well as our weaknesses. They know us inside and out.

My daughter has been an enormous help to me, sometimes just by bringing to my attention how I may not be living up to my potential. She has a lot to learn about the world, being only 22 (going on 35), but she knows the world about me. Our children, with their love for us, their admiration, and their expectations, offer us much help along the road to finding our way back to ourselves.

OURSELVES

Most often, mature women come out of a marriage a bit broken. We no longer trust our instincts, and we often don't recognize our strengths. While it is obvious to us that we are our worst enemy, it should also be obvious to us that we are capable of being our own best resource.

We are the power — the power to steer our lives and make them count. After the healing process, we must make it our job to rebuild the knowledge about ourselves. We must learn who we were, who we are, and who we need to become.

Because there are approximately 43 million women between the ages of 40 and 60, the world is quickly rewriting the rules. Women are adept at dealing with change. A crisis often becomes a challenge or an opportunity. If we don't see it ourselves, we can undoubtedly rely on the women in our lives to bring it to our attention.

We are recognizing that we don't want to go into our later years miserable at our jobs, unhappy in our relationships, or disappointed in ourselves. We hold ourselves accountable. We are often willing to gamble on ourselves. Such a gamble doesn't always come easy, and is often prompted by someone else, but we find that taking a chance on ourselves is never a bad thing.

TAMMY-ISM: *The topic of our gifts is almost spooky. Our gifts are so vast, so strong, so encompassing that it is truly incomprehensible how they go undetected for years. THAT is the mystery, if you ask me. You won't find a bigger believer in inner gifts than me: it ties directly into faith, faith being that belief in something you cannot see. You may not see your gifts, but the chances are pretty good they speak to you. If you are unaware of your gifts, take their existence seriously. It is your obligation to find them, tap into them and live them. I'm not sure of the punishment, if there is any, for not taking steps to seek out our gifts and utilize them, but I don't think I would want to find out. Living our gifts is not an option. It is the unwritten commandment.*

LOVE LOST
IS LIFE FOUND

Hell begins on the day when God grants us a clear vision of all that we might have achieved, of all the gifts which we have wasted, of all that we might have done which we did not do...for me the conception of Hell lies in two words: too late.

- GIAN-CARLO MENOTTI

I t is an undeniable truth that you cannot find what you did not know was lost. Along the way in our relationships, we give away pieces of ourselves. Our motives often are noble; but nevertheless, we find ourselves at the end of the road of our marriage with less in our basket than when we began.

We have less trust, less patience, and less time to waste. However, we must now take the time to find that which we forfeited along the roadside and get it back. It is ours, and we will need it again. And so, we go to the lost-and-found of ourselves and begin to retrieve.

What we find is that our experience from love lost is immeasurably beneficial. It has given us the strength to judge what is right for us and, more importantly, what is wrong. It is essential that we use this strength. I truly believe that every woman has an inner voice and that she spends much of her time squelching it to the best of her ability.

Now, after learning to lose at love and suffering the loss and surviving stronger, we have hopefully learned to listen to that voice. We know to seek it out.

For every woman who has experienced love lost, there is a time when we realize how much better we are for having loved and then having let go. For some, it takes longer than for others, but when the smoke of hurt dissipates, we find ourselves standing on higher ground. It is, however, foreign territory, and it is in the persevering that we become who we were meant to be, who we knew we were all along: happy, strong, independent, successful women.

At the end of love, we all feel a bit cheated. It is inescapable. We say things to ourselves such as: Why me? I deserved more! It wasn't supposed to be like this. All the sentiments of the heart speak truth, but with a biased voice. Love chooses no favorites in its coming and going. To expect otherwise leaves us bitter and disillusioned.

Divorce or death of the spouse we once pledged to love eternally is not what we expected or planned for. It's not only all right to be angry about it, but it's also healthy. Everything has its time slot, its place in our day to day, including anger and bitterness. If allowed to fester, these sentiments will disable us; recognizing this will save us a world of hurt. There is a time to listen to the heart and a time to listen to the head. The time after the initial grieving period is a time for the latter.

If we play our cards right, we might want to thank our ex-husbands for all that they taught us. There is a price to pay for everything, and no one comes out of a relationship unchanged or unhurt. If you think your story of woe and hurt is more tragic than anyone else's, it's time you got over yourself. There is always another woman who suffered more indignity, more financial loss, and more heartache than you.

That is not to say that the loss you have endured is in any way less important or less unique, but rather that it is happening every day to thousands of us. It is not in the retelling of our miseries that we become stronger, better people: it is in the listening, sharing, learning and helping each other through the process.

Now, today, this minute, you are single. If you do not like where you are, you have work to do. The fact that you are unmarried and past 50 signifies a freedom you need to discover.

If you see yourself as alone, what you should be seeing is someone unencumbered.

If you see yourself as incapable, what you should be seeing is someone who is unchallenged.

If you see yourself as limited, what you should be seeing is someone who has yet to tap into her creativity and imagination.

If you see yourself as fearful, you have not yet come to terms with your abilities.

If you see yourself as powerless, you have not recognized your strengths.

It is clear to all of us who have lived through it; that once we stop the whining, crying, and regretting, we can find much better use for our energy. It's the natural course of things. Oh, we may still cry from time to time; hurt runs deep. And we may still experience regret, but it cannot be all that is on our plate. We replace regret with dreams of the future, hopes for success, and plans to make things happen.

THE EX

The most common feeling most women have about their ex-spouses is that they should be covered in honey, buried from the neck down in the desert, and left to die a miserable death. While it is completely natural to have those feelings, this state of mind needs to be temporary. If it isn't, suffice it to say it is we who are in need of some heavy-duty counseling.

In time, if we act with wisdom, we forge a friendship with the men with whom we once chose to spend our lives. This goal is critical when children are involved, no matter their ages, but it is critical for us as well. This friendship may not be the best friend, goody-goody kind of relationship, but it should be strong and reliable.

It took two years for me to reach that point with my former high school sweetheart and husband of 25 years. I don't think I ever worked harder at anything. It was maddening, bitter and satisfying all at once. My ultimate motivation was the realization that I loved my daughter more than I hated my ex-husband. The rest just fell into place.

Even now, when I truly wish him happiness, there is the underlying gut feeling that I cannot shed that says loudly, I should be happy first! And in a perfect world (that exists only in my mind), that would be the case. But it's not a perfect world, and it's not a race. Making peace with that has brought many a good night's sleep. Fighting it only gives us angst, sadness and feelings of despair.

The truth is, we no longer want our husbands. We just don't want anyone else to want them either. That would mean that someone else is benefiting from his mistakes with us, and that is against the unspoken creed of womanhood. While it all makes sense in our heads, and we feel just and righteous in our attitudes, we need to acknowledge that the men we date and select to share our lives with made mistakes in past relationships and, we hope, learned from them. It is then that we find ourselves in the very position we once so strongly resented: we are the one reaping benefits from some other woman's pain. It all comes full circle.

Of course, every woman thinks her tale of woe regarding her ex-husband cannot be topped. But from the stories that have been shared with me, I caution you not to make that assumption.

My divorce, I now believe, was rather run of the mill. I hated his guts, I wished him dead, he cancelled my credit cards, the house went into foreclosure, the utilities were turned off—pretty much the standard fare. Neither of us was unfaithful. Rather, I found myself completely unhappy, and he found himself completely uncaring of that fact. It ended long before I asked him to leave. I cried myself a river, felt neglected, unloved, and misunderstood. I blamed him for not loving me enough to try, and I blamed myself for settling. In the end, it was I who was responsible for me, plain and simple. And it was I who mustered the courage to take a stand and walk away.

My ex-husband was not my most favorite person on earth, but the one unavoidable fact I could not escape was that he was the father of my most precious daughter. For that reason alone, I knew I would have to come to terms with letting go, moving on, and keeping this man as a friend. Forgiveness is key. Without it we are just play-acting.

Today, my ex and I have forged a solid friendship. We talk once or twice a week, and have dinner at least once a month with our daughter. We share stories of work and health ailments and laugh once in a while about the old times we shared. The hurt feelings, anger, and disappointment have not vanished. Once in a while they may rear their ugly heads. We are only human. But, for the most part, we keep them in check, remembering that our past was not completely comprised of bitter memories.

When he suffered a life-threatening motorcycle accident while vacationing in Las Vegas, I flew down to his hospital bed and took care of him. I found him with a few broken ribs, a broken collarbone, and one less spleen. I brought him to my home and put him up in the guest bedroom. There he stayed for two weeks until I could hire home care for him.

I found myself in the unexpected position of wanting to be a friend who was just taking care of another friend. I was, and am, no longer in love with him, but we have been friends since I was 15 years old, and friendships seem to mean more to me these days.

Things had not ended well for us, but I refuse to think that it was all a waste of time. In him, I have an old, high school friend and a father to my child. Those things, in and of themselves, present too much value to just throw away.

When a marriage ends, we lose a partner. Why do we also have to lose the friend we once had? Ultimately, the decision to maintain a friendship is a joint one. I am thankful he was wanting and willing to make our lasting friendship a reality.

It was I who decided to end the marriage after 25 years. It was also I who pursued the friendship with my ex. I would be hard-pressed to tell you which of these tasks was harder. But in life, with its proverbial forks in the road, I could not have made a better decision. The rewards are visible in my daughter's face every day. This gratifies my soul.

To know that the loss of my marriage did not result in the loss of a good friend has been, in the end, a blessing to me. Isn't it interesting the things we learn about ourselves along the way? Love lost is life found.

The trick is in the letting go and moving forward. When I look at him now, I know why I loved him a long time ago. More importantly, I know why I no longer do.

MY GOODBYE

The house was sold, and the furnishings moved out. All that was needed now was a quick once over to be sure nothing of value was left behind.

I drove up to the big house to gather the leftovers of a life packed up and moved, and to do a little sprucing and cleaning of the place. I didn't want the new owners to think I was a messy housekeeper. It made about as much sense as cleaning the house before the cleaning woman comes so she doesn't think you're a slob.

It was a long drive up that damn hill, the same hill I had cursed so many a snowy day, but today was different. I appreciated the surrounding mountains, the herds of deer lingering in the street, and how the sky and clouds seemed to touch the pavement.

I knew this last visit would hold no sadness for me. No regret. Anyone who knew me during this time knew how I had longed to be free of the grand house and its burdens. I'm quite sure there was substantial whining on my part as I waited not too patiently for the house to sell. It took two years.

As I entered, the house was bare of all furniture, dust bunnies lay around in contradiction to my good housecleaning ethics, and it all felt so cold. No sadness, no regret.

I scurried throughout with a duffel bag picking up odds and ends: a dog ball, light bulbs, a stuffed animal, a pot. In the stillness I could swear I could hear my daughter Amanda's youthful voice call out "Mama." I looked in the corner of the kitchen nook and saw our Lab puppy, Sadie, in her dog bed with Amanda crouched in with her. They were both holding onto each other and watching me as I moved us into this big house. I looked out to the vacant backyard and heard the squeals of little girls in the hot tub. I saw the winter snowball fights and the summer water balloon wars. The kitchen was suddenly filled with friends and loud laughs, jokes, and toasts. And I could see my old cat Figgy lying on the heating grate hogging all the heat. My eyes swelled with tears.

I gingerly made my way upstairs and stood in Amanda's bedroom, listening to all the bedtime stories we shared with each other as we looked up through her moon window to the stars in the sky. The tears, the drama, the growing up… of both of us.

It all happened in this house. It felt as though this old house knew all my secrets and loved me anyway. It bore witness to all that had happened and stood silently by me. It felt like it was my friend. And I was leaving it in disarray and disrepair, not at all how to treat a friend. But it is only a house, I kept reminding myself. Only a house.

And then I felt the slightest tug of a memory of my happier life with my ex-husband, Rob. A memory of our pure love and of our promises to each other that ended with broken hearts. I felt a darting pain in my chest. There would be no happily ever after for me here. No having the rooms filled with my grandbabies. No growing old in the house that offered so much promise. It was all done, all over now.

I lost my loving animals Sadie, Punkin, and Figgy in this house. It had seen my heartaches, listened to my sobs. It bore witness to my life for thirteen years. And so, I wondered; is it ever really possible to close a door and feel no sadness, no regret? Even if you think, or know, you are ready to meet what the future brings, does it mean we shouldn't hold tightly to the past and all that it walked us through?

I was confused. Maybe startled would be a better word. I did not expect this reaction, not even a little bit. I went through each room, each closet, making sure a memory was not left behind. I know this sounds crazy, but the house looked and felt sad and lonely. I was compelled to say out loud the comforting words that a new family, children, new drama, new stories would soon consume it, as well as new carpets, countertops, and a nice, new paint job. What the hell was I doing talking to a house? It wasn't the house that needed to hear it, of course; it was me.

And so I grabbed a discarded, old stained Polaroid of Amanda, Rob, and me taken the week we moved into the house, and I left. I drove slowly down that long hill. And I had in my heart sadness, and yes, some regret.

Change is good, but it rarely comes easily. I guess saying goodbye, even to a house is tough. I've come to the conclusion that while endings are imperative for our growth, they sting. Not the kind of sting one soon forgets. A closed door leads to a new path. A good thing I think.

My direction is facing forward, of that I am sure. I am focused on making new memories, having new love, and experiencing wonderful new adventures. Still, I must confess, there is a little piece of me, my kid, my dog, my cats, my former life and love that I left behind when I closed the door and drove down the hill for the last time. It is all just a memory now.

TAMMY-ISM: *Girlfriend, I could talk for days on this subject, but to put it all in a nutshell, I say that we need to admire the shark. Yes, you heard me, the shark. Sharks do not move backwards—they are incapable of the action. It's always forward, never backward, sometimes with lightening speed, sometimes lumbering slowness, but always forward.*

Lost love hurts. We cry because we are wounded. It is not a mortal wound. We learn something each time, something we will need for our future, something that will make our life better. Bet on it. Once it's learned, we need to move forward.

Oh, and just for the record, I don't think it's a bad thing to admire the shark for its ability to eliminate its enemy with cunning speed. A girl's gotta have her dreams.

EMPTY NESTING
IS FOR THE BIRDS

Making a decision to have a child—
it's momentous. It is to decide forever to have
your heart go walking around outside your body.

– Elizabeth Stone

A PERSONAL STORY

At first we go a little crazy, or in my case, a lot crazy. I can tell you that while I thought I was ably prepared to pack my one and only daughter off to college,

I was far from it. You plan with your kids, get excited for them, and prepare yourself for them to leave, and then... it's very quiet. Whether you're sending off your only child, your firstborn, or the last of your brood, their going can leave an empty spot so deep in your life that it's difficult to cope. Suddenly the house seems cavernous. The phone doesn't ring as much, the neighborhood kids aren't piling into your den, and the drama has left the building.

It would appear that most of us need an attitude adjustment during this time in our lives. It felt like I had just lost my best job of the past 18 years, as well as my best friend. I was, in fact, entering a new predetermined phase of life kicking and screaming. It wasn't pretty.

We learn so much about ourselves when the very people we raised leave us. We learn that we are weak and strong at the same time. We learn that we have to face every day and make it work. We learn, finally, that WE are the most important person in our lives. Then we begin to shed our skins. We become new. Some of us take longer than others. But then a miracle occurs. We get over it.

Suddenly, I started to notice that my grocery bill was half as large. My laundry loads shot down to a few times a month. My house stayed cleaner, and I was no longer spending hours in the kitchen preparing for and cleaning up after dinner meals. The music on the CD player was my favorite oldies rather than the current punk band. I had so much more free time. I didn't know what to do with it. Could it possibly be that there was an upside to this situation?

Weeks went by where I would go shopping at the mall for nothing in particular. It was just somewhere to go and something to do. After a month or two of this, I had bought myself a whole new wardrobe. Life as I knew it had changed. And, as it turned out, it wasn't all that bad without my little girl living at home.

My daughter and I kept in touch with at least one phone call every day. I think she was babysitting me during that period. She sensed my fragility without her. She was kind of heart and giving with her stories. It sure didn't hurt to have her on my side. It was a crutch for me, of course—one I found I needed temporarily. I learned what it was like to need my kid the way she had needed me all her life. We both garnered riches from those days. I was, and am, graced with a daughter who cares enough and takes the time to be a bit of a mom to her mom.

IT'S MORE THAN OK

Just when you learn that it's more than okay to live your days and nights for you, you become aware that while kid(s) leave home, they don't leave you. Visits home may be more frequent than you could have imagined. Whenever there is a drama, your phone rings and hours are spent talking and reasoning things out. Laundry loads accompany the adorable little munchkins when they come home to visit. You are treated to late nights, wild friends eating everything not nailed down, and those familiar messes left about. Ah, yes, it all comes back to you rather quickly how wonderful life was when you weren't alone, and how damn good it is now. You're still the mom. Home is still home. The best of both worlds is now yours.

We love our kids more than our lives. The problem for many of us is they became our lives. We submerge our identities with our children, and when they leave, we are left floundering. When we finally let go, we begin learning how to transcend our lives to another plateau. It is our job not only to learn to live without our kids being in our everyday lives, we must learn to love the aloneness.

Friends, hobbies, travel, work, quiet time all help us get through the tunnel. I remember my wonderful aunt trying to prepare me for what she termed the hardest time of her life, her daughter's leaving. She tried her best to talk me through it and help me long distance. She was a blessing. Someone on the other end of the phone understood what I was feeling, and that validated me. I wasn't pathetic. I wasn't abnormal. Her stories encouraged me; her laughter cheered me. She was the only one I had to lean on during that time. It was enough. Her promise to me that I would get through to the other side stronger and more confident was, of course, true.

Sometimes that's all we need, that one person who knows, who understands, and who patiently listens. As women, these things come instinctively to us. What we need, we will seek and find from other women. Nurturing is as natural to women as water is to ducks. It is usually after we have reached a certain age that we discover how to be the nurturer of ourselves. Our children can help us. We are in need of their understanding, love, and yes, sometimes a little advice.

I believe the degree of difficulty in adjusting when our children have left is directly related to the purpose we felt in raising them. For me, my daughter became my purpose for pretty much everything. When she left, I was without a purpose and found myself aimless and confused. I did not recognize my confused state immediately; it only became clear after a good deal of thought and analysis.

Afterwards, I deliberately set out to find a new purpose, and my life got a lot better—happier. My daughter was still my reason for many things, but I became my purpose.

A child is a tug that will last a lifetime. Any mother anywhere in the world will tell you how much she worries about her children. The age of the child is insignificant. My father has in me a 54-year-old daughter, and he still renders advice on how to be safe when I'm out on the streets. Worry is part of the bargain. It's what you get. Learning how to worry less, or perhaps only about those things that are worth our fretting, is an art. I have not reached that goal as yet, but I'm working on it.

The day will come when my daughter will understand the fretful mother's voice on the other end of the line, as well as the occasional panicky call if she doesn't answer her cell at a late hour. It will, of course, be the day that she, herself, is a mother.

Letting go is a bitch, plain and simple. But it is in the letting go that our load is lightened and we are able to fly higher. At first, it will be an effort, a job. But in time, it will become second nature. We are deserving of this time of less obligation. There are no longer little birds in our nest that require daily feedings and protection from the elements. It is just us. And that, my sisters, is a good thing.

MOMS WHO ARE HAPPY TO LET GO

Not all mothers cling to their offspring with desperate abandon. There are some who never experience the sensation of loss when their children leave the home. I have a dear friend who classifies herself as an awful mom because she was relieved to have peace and quiet when her children left the nest. Nothing could be further from the truth.

Those of you who do not have a strong connection with your children do not cease to be wonderful parents. It's different for you, and I believe, you have greatly misunderstood yourselves. Different does not translate to inadequate. A mother who loves her child is a good mother, plain and simple. Circumstances in our lives pull on each of us differently. I know that my friend loves her children with all of her being, yet she did not suffer the empty-nest syndrome upon their departure. But she did suffer guilt for not being like everyone else. To this day she experiences this guilt, and it is my hope for her and for all of you who are similar that you realize and accept that you were a good parent to your children and you did, and do, love them unconditionally.

TAMMY-ISM: *You could write a book on everything I did wrong in this life phase. I'd like to think I'm being too hard on myself but probably not. Hey, I defend myself simply by saying that I tried my best. I'm not sure we can do anything more than that. It's my personal opinion that when our children leave home it is one of the harshest and toughest things to get through. My divorce was easier. I'm still at a loss as to understand exactly why. No matter. With all the mistakes I made along the way, my daughter and I came out stronger and closer. The bond morphed; naturally, we will always be mom and kid, but in addition, we are the best of friends. Letting go was the only thing that enabled me to hang on to something other than my daughter—myself.*

CRADLE TO GRAVE

When I stand before God at the end of my life,
I would hope that I would not have
a single bit of talent left and could say:
I used everything you gave me.

- ERMA BOMBECK

The fact that we are not immortal is a blessing. Trust me on this. The old adage that life is too short is true for some. That it is too long for others is also true. If our time clock were not ticking, if we had eternity to achieve and accomplish, would we? Death gives meaning to life; it gives value and importance to our years. As Lou Erickson so eloquently put it: "Life is like a taxi. The meter just keeps ticking whether you are getting somewhere or just standing still."

It is my belief that many women see their goals achieved at a mature age, not so much because we are so wise and experienced, but because we have garnered some guts. We have thought out the notion that our time on this planet is limited. It marches on, with or without us. After the busy years of child rearing and the marriage experience, the quiet calmness of single life shows us clarity. This is it. We are alone with ourselves. And so, we must act.

I won't bore you with the nothing ventured, nothing gained mentality. What I would rather do is challenge you to admit to yourself that life is about winning. The question is: What does winning mean to you?

This is so important for you to get right. Winning isn't about making more money than your ex nor having a bigger house than your friends. The real meaning of winning is how you feel about your life today, and your present level of happiness. What does your heart tell you about those things that have been left unlived and undone? Winning is living and doing those things. It could be as simple as wishing you had spent more time with your family, or been more adventurous, traveled more, ridden a horse, or started a business. It could be, and is, a million things.

Let's do an exercise. Imagine yourself with just a few hours to live. You are comfortable in your bed in your home. You are surrounded by the world you made for yourself, the family and friends that you love and don't want to leave. You are faced with the end of your life, and you have the need to speak words of gratitude and regret. What would they be? Your thoughts of gratitude are what you did right in your life. Your regrets are what you got wrong. Now imagine that in that final moment of that final hour, you were given a gift of more time. What would you do with it? If you are like most of us, you'd promise yourself you would spend every moment living to the fullest. By doing so, you would overcome your fears and your excuses. That is winning!

Winning in the game of life, being happy and self-assured is what it is all about. As Leo Durocher, the famous baseball manager, once said: "Show me a good loser, and I'll show you an idiot." I agree. Ultimately, it's all about choice. Being brave enough to choose a path that may be least expected of you, because you are aware of the happiness it could bring, is winning in and of itself. In the end it's about courage and confidence or the lack thereof.

Perhaps the pitfall in life is not being willing to risk anything. If you don't risk, you don't do anything, you don't achieve anything. If you are trying to avoid failure, misery, and heartache, you may succeed. But beware. You will also avoid success, happiness, and love, as well as unrequited peace of mind and soul.

Find your passion and then pursue it. I truly believe we were all born with a combination of gifts exclusive to us. Our task is to figure out what those gifts are. For many of us, it takes a long time to find purpose. Some miss the mark completely. But when we find our gifts, if we are brave, we spend the rest of our lives using them. Marilyn Greist stated it best when she said, "Your passion is waiting for your courage to catch up." Amen!

DO YOU KNOW YOUR EXPIRATION DATE?

The passing of years and the unknowing of our own expiration date is a startling recommendation by life itself to live it happily. We so often settle into jobs we don't like for the paycheck, relationships that fall dreadfully short for the security of having someone there, and a life less lived because we were simply too busy to give it much thought.

After going for a mammogram, I was notified about a mass in my right breast. As any woman would react, I panicked. After going for a diagnostic mammogram, I was notified that a biopsy would be necessary in order to determine if the mass was cancerous. More panic.

I waited a week for the biopsy appointment, imagining the worst, and figuring in my head how I would provide for my daughter after I was gone. Sorrow, distress, sadness, and sheer unmitigated fear took over my days and nights. That is the bad side of things.

The good side of things is the immediate appreciation I felt for those things around me that went unnoticed in the many years before. I walked my little dog Maddy every day, but somehow, that week I was keenly aware of the cool breeze in the air, the smell of coming rain, the clouds, the sky, the peacefulness of the woods around us. I noticed this because, in my mind, I knew there was a possibility that I would be six feet under in the near future.

Everything became clearer, brighter, more significant. It was a beautiful realization, and one I still regret not having before. This realization is one I will carry with me every day.

The news from the biopsy was good, and life gave me a reprieve. I no longer thought of myself as being a step away from my grave since my life had not been given its termination date. And then the question presented itself to me: How did I know I wasn't going to die tomorrow from some unknown occurrence? I realized that I do not know when my expiration date is, and while I'm hopeful I have lots and lots of time left on my clock, I have sadly witnessed a good many of my friends' and peers' lives end. I doubt very much that they expected it or saw it coming.

And so it sparked in me the realization that today, this week or next, may be my last here on this great planet. While I became appreciative of many of life's little blessings, I also became very angry.

If this was going to be my last six months on this earth, then why the hell was I spending it working daily in a job I disliked, for pay that was inadequate, and for little or no appreciation of my contribution? There was always talk about changing jobs, moving on, doing this and accomplishing that, talk that took place at the seat in front of my desk where I performed the job that I hated, day, after day, after day. This was unacceptable! That old saying we toss around so glibly that life is too short is the somber truth. Life is too short, and the real glitch in that over used saying is that none of us knows exactly how short it will be.

So living a life of contentment is essential. Not just relaxing, traveling or whatever suits your happiness quota, but your day-to-day job needs to be doing something that you will not look back on as a waste of your time, talent and gifts. If I said to you today, "I'm sorry to share this with you, but you have ten months, one week and five days left of your life," would you reassess and change how you spend your days? The answer most of us would give is a loud and sadly resounding YES!

TAMMY-ISM: *Take NOTHING for granted. You may not get another chance, another day. None of us wake up in the morning thinking and knowing that this will be our last day on Earth. And yet, one of our mornings that statement will ring true. And so I would encourage you to take chances, be purposeful, laugh at your self, be generous and sincere, and for the love of all that is holy, go have some fun in your life.*

DATING

One should always be in love.
that is the reason one should never marry.

- OSCAR WILDE

It is a general consensus that dating sucks. Most of us haven't done it in years, and it is more than likely many of us haven't a clue how to go about it. Dating, the ways and methods often conjured in our minds, usually involves a bar or a restaurant bar scene. While that may work for some, it is not the answer for most. It's no wonder women cringe at the thought of having to be out on the prowl in order to meet a suitable companion. Here is the good news: that is not how the mature woman dates.

According to AARP (2006) Foundation's Women's Leadership Circle Study of 2,500 women, the mature single finds their dates in the following ways:

41% from referrals from friends, family, and neighbors

20% from the workplace

13% (1 in 7 of us) chat in public places, such as the market, coffee shops

13% in nightclubs and bars

12% at church

12% hobby-related events, such as dancing, gardening

10% traveling

9% doing sports activities

9% attending community activities

9% online dating, and single's groups and organizations

It has been my observation that the most favorable way to meet someone is to be out and about. I have not heard of one instance where a man knocked on a woman's door announcing his arrival and availability. Put yourself in a target-rich environment that suits you. If you like to read, go to bookstores, book readings, and join a club. If you love dogs, join activities involving your pet. Even going to the park can result in meeting someone of interest.

However, I am strongly against the notion that women should join groups or activities for the sole purpose of meeting men. What a waste of time. Attend those functions that interest you and give you pleasure, whether you meet a man or not. This is your free time, and it's about you and what makes you happy. It is not a hunt, but I assure you, if you don't stick your nose out of the house once in a while, it's unlikely you will be socially active anytime soon.

Dating successfully as a mature single is easier than you may imagine. We are far too old and far too wise to play silly time-consuming games. We have earned the right to be up front and honest. We have earned the right to be ourselves.

THE BASICS

First off, let me be the first one to tell you to stop waiting for Mr. Right. As you may have gathered, he doesn't exist. That's okay because chances are pretty good that you are not perfect either.

It's interesting to note the reasons for dating listed in a recent survey (AARP 2003):

Date to have someone to talk to and do things with: 49%

Date to have fun: 18%

Date to live with someone, but will not marry: 9%

Date to find a marriage partner: 8%

Date to fulfill sexual needs: 6% (Five times as many men (11%) state this as a reason, compared to 2% of the women surveyed.)

An enlightening factoid from this survey showed that only 2% of women stated that sex is acceptable during the first date, while 20% of men think it is. The frustrations surrounding dating were listed as: dating people with baggage, being shy and self-conscious, not knowing where to meet people, dating people who push for a serious relationship too quickly, and dating people who become difficult after the initial few dates.

The feedback garnered only confirms that dating is a process that requires thought, selection, and brutal honesty. When 67% of midlife singles view personality as the leading desirable characteristic and 49% of us follow with the need for common interests, it is evident that, unlike our youthful single counterparts, we are looking in the right direction.

While our dating priorities seem to be in place, it is our job to zone in on the qualities that are most important to us. As an exercise, choose three (non-physical) qualities that you cannot be without in a life partner. When you have given it considerable thought, should any of those three qualities be absent in a potential suitor, view it as a red flag to pass. <u>No exceptions</u>.

Now, zone in on three physical qualities (or characteristics) that you could not tolerate under any circumstances in a life partner. Should any of these qualities exist in any potential partner, again, pass. <u>No exceptions</u>.

Don't be in a hurry. Where's the fire? Don't worry, you're still smoldering. Just don't feel compelled to prove it to yourself by being prematurely sexual with someone who is unworthy. You are better than that, and you need to have a lot more consideration and respect for yourself. You will be sexually active again. Give yourself time. Lots of it.

BAGGAGE

Baggage is good. Golden! Show me a man that doesn't have it, and I'll show you a man who hasn't learned a damn thing. The term "baggage" is highly overused. We consider it a bad thing, a detriment. Our girlfriends tell us to steer clear of the man who has too much baggage; he's clearly too much trouble, too much work.

You need to understand that you are also the carrier of some substantial baggage. Baggage is what makes us who we are. It explains us. The more you know about a person's baggage, the more capable you are in determining if you are able to understand and accept them. Whoever said, what you don't know won't hurt you, was a blithering idiot. It is in the *not* knowing that we blindly sail into troubled waters.

If knowledge is power, then make it your business to learn about a potential companion's baggage. And, when the time is appropriate, share some of yours. Hiding secrets is not a good recipe for a workable, happy relationship.

In short, baggage should be rummaged through, weighed, and examined closely. It is an explanation of your present state and a road map of where not to drive. Age brings with it an advantage in the reading of the road map of a potential partner's baggage when it is laid open for you. Stop, yield, proceed with caution, merge, and speed limits, all make themselves visible to both partners when personal baggage is shown and shared.

In essence, baggage, yours or his, is history. It's the life story of a road traveled. It is something we should want to know more about. Quick judgments and assumptions have no place in the dating arena. Unless you are prepared to be sized up and quickly judged by your past actions or mistakes, take caution not to do the same. Being too judgmental could easily cost you a wonderful relationship.

This brings us to sharing. We all learned at a very young age that sharing is commendable, caring, and expected. In embarking on new relationships, there can be some danger here. Our potential partner isn't entitled to know everything about us, our past relationships, or our children. Sometimes, less is more. This is not to say you should withhold important and vital information, but take your time getting out of the gate with the story of your life, and make sure that the man you are spending time with meets your standards before private issues are shared too openly.

Be open-minded. This is easier said than done, especially for the woman over 50. We are notoriously known to be set in our ways. Repeat after me, change is good.

Love has many faces. Some men who may be very compatible with you may be less tall than you might expect or have less hair. They may be all country while you are all city. The answer here is a resounding, so what? One of the advantages at our age is being able to say that we have finally figured out what is really important in a person. If you are still hung up on a full head of hair or a six-pack abdomen, it is probably time you took stock of what matters. I also invite you to take a good, hard look in the mirror. It's sometimes much harder to accept what is looking back at you, than your memories of who you once were. Give it some thought. An open mind leads to an open heart. And an open heart usually leads to found love.

Sadly, there are no knights on white horses. There is no one who is waiting to save you. You, my friend, like me, are all you have to depend on. Sound hopeless? Ah, I think not! Who better to have guarding your gate, watching your step, seeking viable friendships and love-mates, than the person who knows your needs best? You, of course. Who needs knights in shining armor when you are the beautiful queen of hearts with the ability to choose your own mate on your own terms?

Waiting for the man to make the first move or show the first sign of interest is a waste of your time. This isn't our parent's generation. It is absolutely okay for women to invite a male friend for coffee or a movie. For many in our age group, this kind of action seems almost unfathomable.

Get over it! It's a new day, and the rules we women play by have gotten so much better. Your destiny lies in the direction you steer it, but you have to get in the car first!

The sad and obvious truth is men have lost a lot of their mojo by the time they have reached our age. They have been rejected, dejected, misguided, misjudged, embarrassed, and left hanging out to dry. Granted, many of these situations may have been due to the man pursuing someone way out of his age group, or perhaps his behavior at the time warranted rejection. Whatever the reasons, men do not generally come to terms with the aging-and-being-single process as easily as many of their female counterparts.

As a member of the female population, I am a huge fan of the female gender. However, I must say out loud what many of us know. Women can be bitches, and many a man has been laid flat by an insulting comment or a keenly manipulative act rendered by an angry woman. Male egos are bruised far more easily, and their confidence is shattered with little effort. Keep that in mind when you are waiting for that special interest to finally step up to the plate and ask you to dinner. Give him encouragement. Give him an invitation. Life will go so much more smoothly when you take the wheel of the romance ship.

TEN THINGS YOU NEED TO
KNOW ABOUT DATING

1. Take your time. Take it slow.

2. Remember your self-respect. Don't go anywhere without it.

3. Keep your expectations realistic. It's a date, not a marriage proposal.

4. Be yourself. (Isn't that what our mothers always told us?) And don't talk about your ex.

5. Be fair, be kind, but above all, be honest.

6. Sex has no place in the first-phase dating relationship.

7. Share your interests, goals, and likes, and be willing to listen to his. Don't waste your time on inquiring about his hometown or the weather. Ask the questions that are important for you to know, while making sure it is not an inquisition.

8. Keep your antenna up (i.e., he wants kids, he hates animals, he doesn't believe in monogamous relationships). Alarm signals differ for all of us, but it's vital to be aware of any signals sent your way that would make you incompatible.

9. Never suffer rudeness. If you did not drive yourself, always take cab fare just in case you want to leave without him. Depend on yourself.

10. Be open-hearted and open-minded. Only then will you allow good things to come your way.

Be clear in your mind what it is you are looking for. Sounds easy, but it becomes a bit more complicated when you are forced to give the matter serious thought. And the matter of dating does indeed warrant serious consideration by you.

By contrast, I was told by a good friend of mine who is 55 years young and divorced for the last six years that it was easier for her to pinpoint those attributes she didn't want in a companion than it was for her to outline what she was seeking. It works for her, and it might work for you. The point is, think it out. Have an idea of what you believe makes you happy in a relationship. It will make the entire dating experience more enjoyable and fruitful.

As women, we must be vigilant. An attentive eye is always needed in matters of the heart. Whatever you're looking for, it pays to be careful.

Make smart decisions. If you don't know the potential date, don't have him come to your home. Rather, make a date for coffee and meet him there. If you have a gut feeling that something is not right, listen to your feelings. Instincts are God's gift to us. It would be pure folly not to listen to them. Guard yourself. Don't give out your phone number freely, and ask your friends to follow this rule. And please, don't dress provocatively simply to impress. If it impresses him, it doesn't speak well of his intentions. Use sound judgment. In short, follow the advice you gave to your children when they ventured out into the world. A little caution never hurt anyone.

ONLINE DATING SERVICES

Dating services are a viable option. Online dating has gotten a bad rap, but stories have emerged of happy unions resulting from it. The online dating venue has proven itself to be one of the fastest growing industries in our time. Two out of every five single people have tried it. No longer thought of as a last resort or reserved for losers and geeks, online dating has become mainstream and offers some opportunities that cannot be matched. Where else can you browse, greet, and chat with single people wearing your robe and fuzzy slippers?

I have been a participant in the process and can report firsthand that it can be both frustrating and rewarding. One thing it isn't is dull. Online dating provided me with possibilities my otherwise busy schedule would not allow. It appeals to my sensibilities, as my goal is to have some socialization with like-minded people, rather than locating my perfect match.

I prefer to be up-front in relationships. This venue affords me the luxury of stating how I feel about issues that are important to me even before I meet him. While I like the functionality of the online dating process, it isn't always fabulous. I speak from experience when I say that online dating is similar to other methods; it harbors the good, the bad, and the ugly. If you are able to cut to the chase, read between the lines, and stop communication when red flags appear, you are ahead of the game.

It's important to remember that as much as online dating services broadcast their concern and caring for those of us seeking companionship, it is a business, an extremely lucrative and competitive business. It is likely that their major concern lies in our renewal of their subscription. The choice of dating sites offers a varied menu of interests. Are you a dog lover? Looking for religious similarities? It is all out there in cyberspace awaiting your participation.

If you choose to pursue this method of dating, proceed with optimism, eagerness and caution. While most offer extensive bio pages that provide you with interesting and important facts about your potential match, not all participants may be as truthful as they should be.

If you view online dating as a starting point, I don't think you will be disappointed. If you view it as the answer to your prayers for finding a mate, I fear you will be *terribly* disappointed. Never lose sight of the fact that finding the ideal person to share your life with is a process that requires time and patience. It has to start somewhere, and online dating offers an avenue not available to previous generations. It can turn out to be your springboard to finding love.

Shyness and being self-conscious have been cited as the second-highest frustration in dating. An Internet connection can help bypass these factors, as you are able to communicate before actually meeting. The value of this method is ultimately your call. Obviously, the goal of Internet dating is to get off the net and meet in person. Credibility, sincerity, and compatibility are all qualities that cannot be truly judged on a computer. Neither can chemistry. The bottom line is this: it is the face to face, the personal conversation, and the look in the eye that will tell you what you want to know. Positive attitude, vigilant caution, and reasonable expectations will reap the greatest benefits.

This is a good time to directly address the issue of paranoia. I happen to subscribe to the school of thought that if you are a bit paranoid about someone, you may have good reason. When meeting people on the Internet, you lack the advantage of a personal and trusted referral. For example, if a friend, family member or coworker wishes to introduce you to a man, you have built-in, somewhat verifiable, data before going out on the date. With Internet dating, you are flying blind and relying on instinct and common sense.

If you have had a few dates with a man you consider high potential, and you are thinking of taking it to the next level, proceed with caution. You would not be out of line in considering hiring one of the many services available to conduct a background check on the man of interest. The ability to verify marital status, workplace, birth date, and various other important details is at your disposal, and should be a tool commonly used by the Internet dater.

Consider this source as a replacement for the personal referral you would have received had you met them through a friend. This is yet another instance where knowledge is power. Life may be a gamble, but dating shouldn't hold high risks. These services can usually be found in your local phone book or Internet search engine, usually under the listing of private investigator. Services can range anywhere from twenty five dollars to a few hundred, depending on what you request.

A good attitude goes a long way toward getting you what you want. Do not view mismatches as rejections. That is a common and ruinous mistake. One of the dangers we all face is feeling a connection to someone who may not feel the same for us. You will not like everyone you meet, and everyone you meet will not like you. While it may be hurtful and maddening, it is not a rejection. It is simply not the connection you thought it was or hoped it would be. Understanding yourself and your needs is key in the dating arena. If you compromise your desires, you compromise yourself, plain and simple.

Don't be fearful of heart. It's natural to feel a bit scared before your first date. You will most likely have many first dates. Look forward to them. Look at them as opportunities. Our wisdom of age and experience offers us tremendous instinctual abilities. We have but to listen to these instincts.

It's fun to be social. It's fun to dress up a bit and feel pretty. It's fun to meet new people, go to new places. Remember, you are not desperate; you are there because you want to be. You will meet interesting men and women with whom you share common interests, and your life will be richer for it. It's funny how things work out. The more interesting you are, the more interesting the people you connect with become. Coincidence? Not at all. Birds of a feather do flock together.

There is no shortage of books on the subject of dating. Some are by famous TV personalities, some by self-proclaimed experts, and others by psychologists. A little insight and advice on how to deal in the real world of dating is never a bad thing. Just never forget that YOU are the best authority for knowing what works best for you.

THE COUGAR

Today, the term "cougar" often refers to the woman who is exclusively looking to hook up with a much younger man. Personally, I find the term offensive. I have never been a fan of double standards. Women who favor the companionship of younger men are generally not predators, prowlers or hunters. If you are a woman in your forties, fifties, or sixties looking for male companionship years younger than yourself, I believe firmly that this is your right and your business.

A recent survey conducted for *AARP the Magazine* tells us that 34% of women between the ages of 40 and 69 are dating younger men (Mahoney 2003). I find it disturbing that no one makes a fuss when an older man dates, marries, or impregnates a woman half his age. What's good for the gander is good for the goose.

One-third of older, single women are dating a younger partner. There are many advantages cited by older women as to why younger men may suit their needs better than men their own age. A woman of age has much to offer. Her most alluring quality is confidence. Younger men are attracted to confidence like a moth to a flame.

The younger man is far less likely to want to sit on the couch with the TV remote in his hand and more likely to want to go out and dance, dine, travel, and just have fun.

Younger men may also offer the attraction of no strings attached. Mature women appreciate that factor, as men their own age are often compelled to push their ideal of marriage into play. The younger man also benefits from this agreed arrangement. They appreciate the experience and maturity of an older woman and have the benefit of sharing a life with someone who does not share their generation's hang-ups, challenges, and fears.

Many of us have spent a lifetime being married, and while it was hopefully wonderful for us, we have been there and done that. Most women 50 years and over married quite young and did not afford themselves the experience of dating and sampling life from different menus. This is our chance to date, experience new people, new places, new feelings, and new challenges.

I spent the better part of 25 years in the company of another human being 24/7. I have barely scratched the surface of what makes me happy. Marriage may have had its space and time in all our lives. Now, it's time to be a bit selfish. Yes, we welcome the idea of sharing our lives with a wonderful man, but we don't need to compromise our wants, needs, and desires in exchange for the opportunity.

This time around, this second life you've been handed, is about you, and for you. Younger men can be far more attentive and accepting. You cannot control gossip, nor should you let gossip control you. Oh, and one last thing. If someone disapproves, *it ain't nobody's business but yours!*

OPTION B—NOT DATING

A surprising number of mature, single women have chosen not to date. A "lifestyles, dating, and romance" study of midlife singles surveyed 3,501 single men and women between the ages of 40 and 69. The study found that 14% would date if the right person happens to come along, but otherwise were not interested in participating in the dating arena. Another 9% declared they were not interested in dating at all (AARP 2003).

The reasons sited for this decision was threefold. First, they simply like their lives just as they are and have no desire to change them. Secondly, too many bad experiences with past relationships have left their imprint. Thirdly, they felt that relationships presented too much trouble and effort.

It is a monolithic misinterpretation that the woman who has made the conscious decision to refrain from dating is bitter, lonely, and without purpose. I have spoken to many women who have chosen to reject the option of dating at this time in their lives, and can report to you unequivocally that these women are not, by any stretch of the imagination, women of low esteem or substandard in any way. The contrary is true. These women are vibrant, attractive, confident individuals who have created a life for themselves that is happy and fulfilled. Generally, they lead busy lives involving work, relationships, travel, and hobbies. They possess an optimistic attitude and giving spirit, and it has been my pleasure to know and count many as my friends.

SEX AND THE SINGLE GIRL

Well, now, here's a touchy subject. Since I am aware that by even opening the topic for discussion, I am bound to offend someone, I say, what the hell, let's talk. The actual number of men I have had sex with in my life isn't overly impressive by some people's standards. The number remains in the single digits. But the quantity and the quality of the sex I have known, well, that *is* impressive. I must confess I didn't waste a moment with any of the loves I have known. I was, and am, an all or nothing girl. Sex is fun. Sex is fulfilling. Sex is good for us. Sex provides the ultimate sharing and intimacy. Where I come from, sharing and intimacy are good things. In short, I am a fan of sex.

Now that I have said that out loud, let me qualify that statement just a bit. Random, meaningless sex for the sake of sex is just what the words imply: random and meaningless. I am not a fan of random, meaningless sex. There is no room in a smart woman's life for this kind of folly. It will often bring with it negative repercussions.

I am also not a fan of having sex for any reason other than you deeply care for and want the person you are with, and have a committed relationship with them. In my opinion, sex is an extension of love, desire, and the need to care for and be cared about.

We shouldn't be having sex with people we barely know or people we are not deeply fond of. It is what separates us from the animals. I may want to be sexual with an amazing man I am talking to because I find him incredibly sensual and intelligent. But I don't. I am not a wild animal acting on basic instinct. I have a thought process, and I use it. What I have to share, what I have to give, is amazing. It is me, in my entirety, and I have immeasurable worth. We all do. The truth is, I have gone long periods of time without the benefit of knowing someone who I believed worth my time, energy and love, but I did not do it sex-less.

The secret that every mature woman knows is that she can have great sex all by herself. Oh, stop judging, and don't look so shocked. It's a natural thing to explore our bodies; most of us have been doing it since we were very young. And let me say, from a personal perspective, I am quite good, a tough act to follow.

I carry no shame in pleasuring myself when the need or desire spurs me. Shame is something that is levied on us by some religious beliefs, and parental expectations. While it is obvious that sex is meant to be shared, the discerning woman is too smart to allow herself to be in a thankless relationship because of her need for sex. Self-gratification is an option, a temporary solution, for those unwilling to sell themselves short.

While sex is an important component in our life, it should always have a discerning voice. Be selective. Be careful. Be sure. Then, be happy. Explore the relationship you have deemed ready for the next step. And I don't care how much you trust him, use a condom. If you love him, want to marry him, know he is the man for you, use a condom. If he swears on his mother's life that he is free of all disease and you are the only woman he has been with in years, use a condom. I think you get the point here. We live in an age where unprotected sex could easily result in sexually transmitted disease. Never, ever take a chance for the sake of sex.

Sex is not always a wanted component in the life of every woman. Some women see it as a duty. You show me a woman who does not enjoy sex, and I'll show you a woman who has been in the company of inexperienced or uncaring sexual partners. If you allow yourself the chance to let someone into your life who knows and loves you for who you are, chances are good he will want to please you. We are called upon to give ourselves another chance to try, to explore, to be open to the idea. If, despite those efforts, you find yourself without any sexual interest or desires and there is no medical reason for the disinterest, and you are not interested in changing, don't. It's your life, it's your call, and you have no one to report to but yourself. Live happy. Sex is a wonderful option, not a command. Just be sure to be open and honest with the men you invite into your world.

What does sex and religion have to do with each other? The answer lies within you and your belief system. If you both are single, willing participants, and have made the decision to be in a committed relationship, well, then, have at it. It is your decision, and yours alone, and I support it. If you wish to follow the teachings of your faith which may advise you to not engage in sex outside of marriage, that is your decision. I support you. The point to be made here is that the mature woman has reached the stage in her life where she knows what is good for her, what works, and what doesn't. She no longer needs to subscribe to ancient values, rigid concepts, or slanted religious biases.

So, let's summarize. Sex is good. Meaningless sex is bad. Finding our own standard and sex life is good. Listening and succumbing to other people's expectations is bad. Having sex with someone you are not monogamous with is bad. Being responsible in our decisions is good, and unprotected sex is very, very bad.

THE "YOU WANT ME TO DO WHAT?" PHASE

Okay, ladies, let's talk nitty-gritty here. The idea of getting naked in front of someone with the lights on can represent paralyzing fear in its ultimate form. Being asked to try different methods, positions, and techniques is something you will most likely encounter—if you're lucky. The answer to happiness is having an open mind, heart, and a good imagination. The sexual arena is no exception. It's important to stand by your standards. It is equally important to be open to listening and considering your partner's desires and needs. Let's hear from some of the girls.

HEATHER

I always wanted to be more adventurous in my sexual activity with my husband, but he was never interested in deviating very much. I never pushed the issue. A few years after my divorce, I met an amazing man that was, shall we say, gifted. He was open, willing, and hell-bent on pleasing me in ways I had never known existed. The problem for me was I wasn't working with my 20-year-old body; I was working with my 54-year-old body. To say I was self-conscious would be an understatement. Eventually, I talked openly to him about my hang-ups, and he worked with me. We made sure the room was only lit by a candle or soft light, and he promised not to probe my body too much with his hands. I am happy to report that I got over my phobias pretty darn fast. Now I want the light on and I place his hands on me. Candles still work nicely, but they are no longer required. Honey, if I can get past it, anyone can!

SABRINA

I remember the first time I had sex with a man after my divorce. I was so nervous I thought I would turn into a ball of sweat. It wasn't easy for me. It wasn't like the movies. I was so concerned about him liking me that I wasn't truthful about my needs. I didn't want to be rejected in the sack, so my one focus was to be liked and wanted back. Obviously, the relationship was all about the sex. What a waste of time. Maybe I'm just one of those people that have to learn the hard way. After he left I thought to myself, I don't need to have unfulfilling sex anymore. That was for married people who often didn't have the option. I <u>did</u> have the option, and I made the decision that night to be honest in my future relationships. I still work to please, but I ask, too. It's a two-way street, and I spent way too many years on the wrong side of it. I wasn't ready for a committed relationship, nor did I think it really went hand-in-hand with sex. I was wrong. Those days are over.

GAYLE

I had been dating this great guy for four and a half months, and we both wanted to take it to the next level...sex. I was hungry for it. It had been three years for me. But I was also pretty mortified at the thought of this wonderful man seeing my cellulite and little love handles. And would he notice that one of my boobs was larger than the other? I gave myself all kinds of excuses, all based on years of insecurities. Then one night, I purposely had two glasses of wine (a lot for me), and I actually told him out loud that I wanted to have sex with him, but I was shy and afraid. Definitely an out-of-character move on my part. It was honest, it was direct, and it was the best thing I could have said. Let's just say that it all worked out great, and I have a new respect for the phrase, the truth shall set you free.

There you have it, ladies. Sex and the single, mature woman are alive and well. Do I hear an Amen?!

TAMMY-ISM: When it comes to dating, if you are waiting for the perfect time, seeking out signs or waiting for your life to be in order, your opportunities will slip away. There is no perfect time, and I have yet to see a sign of any kind. At our age, dating is far less about the hunt and more about the gratification in finding a connection of like minds and souls. Obstacles will present themselves; walk over them. Chances will need to *be taken. Time is your most precious commodity. Use it wisely and with purpose. Woman was not meant to live without the joy of love in her life.*

FAMILY: FURRY
AND OTHERWISE

*Animals are reliable, many full of love,
true in their affections, predictable in their
actions, grateful and loyal. Difficult standards
for people to live up to.*

- ALFRED A. MONTAPERT

Ah, yes, the family: the loyal, dysfunctional, loving, helpful, meddlesome, and supportive bloodline we are born into. The definition of family changes at such a fast pace, it's hard to keep up. Simply because you are related to someone doesn't always assure you of their love and support. In our busy lives, we often find ourselves lacking family. We have all heard the saying you can't choose your relatives, but in effect, we have found a way to do just that. We have created extended family networks consisting of those people we can turn to or lean on when the going gets tough. Or, perhaps we turn to a beloved pet if we just want to hug or receive a wet smooch.

Probably to no one's surprise, many of the most endearing family members are not relatives at all, but rather four-legged friends, our chosen furry companions. Wherever you find them, next door, at work, the animal shelter, your extended family will serve as your comforter, your cheerleader, and your relentless fan.

In these times, many families no longer live in the same state. We have been called upon to improvise. We seek and find those people who we are able to establish a relationship with. People with whom we have a give-and-take and talk-and-listen system that provides each of us with that little extra support we all need from time to time. We become each other's family. It is no coincidence that many popular sitcoms are based on this premise. *Friends, Seinfeld, Will and Grace, Grey's Anatomy,* to name a few, show how a group of un-related people can become family and support each other. From discussions with many of the women I interviewed, this was absolutely the case.

Also from these discussions, I learned how animals play an important role in our family circle. My furry friends are no exception. Here is one such story:

ONE OF MY BEST FRIENDS

Figaro was an amazing cat that didn't know he wasn't human. He offered us unconditional love, understanding, humor, and companionship. When he came to live with us, my daughter was two. She went away to college three years ago. He saw her off and saw me through the adjustment. Figaro shared our lives and was unfazed by its traumas and drama. His answer to life's problems was just to love us through it all. It was the right answer.

Recently I found myself in the dreaded position of having to put my beloved pet of 18 years to sleep. I dropped him off at the vet for some tests, and when I left him there for the morning, I knew in my heart I would not be bringing him home with me. I went back that late afternoon, knowing I would have to say goodbye to my dearest friend for the last time.

When I entered the room, he rose off his little bed to greet me. I hugged him like you hug when you know you will never hug again. I leaned over him and whispered to him how much I loved him and how grateful I was that he found his way into my life. I reminded him of when he brought home a bird as big as a Buick and when he got stuck in the attic and we had to have the siding removed to get him out. I thanked him for his loyalty and love, and told him I was doing the best I knew how for him. I kissed him all over his little head, and he was gone.

My heart broke, and in that moment I knew I had not lost a cat, but a member of my family.

Figgy was not the first animal to grace my life. There was Chopper, Punkin, and Sadie, all of whom left an imprint on my mind and my heart that still brings a smile to my face and tears to my eyes. They helped me through many phases of my life.

FAMILIES ARE NOT ALWAYS BLOODLINE

Family is who we bring into our lives. The people and the animals that enrich us, enable us to carry on, to be better, and to feel loved. The notion that family is exclusive to the bloodline we join at birth is absurd. Family is our support, and we gather our support where we can get it. We weave a basket of relationships along the trail we call life; without those relationships, there would be nothing. In each of our baskets we place beautiful flowers, each important to the bouquet. Our basket, our family, is our life's loves, pains, work, and worth.

Living our lives requires courage, a dash of daring, common sense, and a need to love and be loved and accepted by family. Family nourishes, encourages, and listens. Many would say that the beings in their lives that provide these things are not people at all, but pets. I would not argue. Nor would I argue against the fact that much of the support and acceptance I have received, has been given by the people in my life to whom I have no blood relation. They are that select group of friends that became my family when I wasn't looking. This is not unusual, I'm told. Below are the voices of kindred women.

JULIA

After seven years of marriage, we adopted Max, a terrier mix, from the local animal shelter. Max saw me through the birth of my two children, my depression, my unfaithful husband and my divorce. Only when he was gone did I realize how important he was to me and to the kids. It was like he was the glue that held it all together when things got rough. I don't know how a little, scruffy dog can make you feel worthy when the world tells you otherwise, but he did just that. I love him still, and I would fight anyone to the death who said he was not family.

MISTY

I met Grace, an older, gutsy coworker when I started a temporary job at an accounting office. She was at least 15 years my senior and very proper in every sense of the word. A bit conservative and stiff, I could never have guessed she would prove to be one of the best friends in my life. She took the time to listen, the caring to extend herself, and she gave me wisdom of the ages. I can't say that I always agreed with her opinions, but she was gracious in allowing that we could agree to disagree and still maintain a great friendship. Mostly, she encouraged me to look at myself with higher esteem, something I know to this day I could never have done without her coaxing me. She is more family to me than my natural family. I respect her, I enjoy and need her, but mostly, I love her. When I think of family during the holidays, it is

Grace who comes to mind. We have been the best of friends and had the strongest of family ties to each other for the past dozen years or so. Strange is the glue that binds two people together who are so different, yet so in need of each other.

PAM

I had moved to an apartment after my divorce and encountered someone I perceived to be the neighbor from hell. He was cantankerous, noisy, played awful opera music loudly, and was inclined to monitor my comings and goings. It was a rocky start that ended with my education. In his simplicity, he taught me more about life, humor, and acceptance than I could have ever imagined. Joe was part of my family for seven years. I moved to a lovely town home, and he became a regular visitor and a staple during the holidays. Joe passed away a few months ago from a heart attack. I cannot imagine that I could grieve for him more or miss him any less if he were my blood.

GWENDLYN

I married at 19. I was the older of two children and had never even spent the night away from home before my marriage. Our first week in our apartment a very scraggly cat came meowing at the front porch. He looked worse for the wear, and we gave him a "temporary" home while we searched for his owner. Fourteen years later, I found myself out on my own after a bitter divorce. Because I was unable to conceive, Tiger was my only child. That scraggly cat was now old, but was my truest friend. He offered me comfort and love through those years of tribulation and heartbreak. We went through a lot together, that old cat and I. Words fail me when I try to describe how heartbreaking it was for me when he died. I look back on those years, and I remember the many times Tiger brightened my days. I'm 56 years old now, and I still think of that little scraggly cat and the positive difference he made in my life. Was he like family to me, you ask? You bet your ass he was.

FROM MY PAST

A small chapter from my past: I remember my grandfather's last days many years ago. He was a tough old bird, but had been confined to a wheelchair for the last dozen years. A soft-spoken man and a commercial fisherman by trade, he had a striking, independent nature. Most of his friends had passed away before him, and he was, for the most part, isolated from the real world. He adopted a stray cat in his last years and they became the best of friends.

Grandpa was always anxious to share stories of silly things his cat had done. In his last days, he was on a feeding tube and had another tube in his throat to help him breath. He was sent home to die—his request. That big, old, fat cat would sit on Grandpa's chest, and we would be mortified at the mere weight of the animal on his fragile body. He would bark at us if we attempted to lift the cat off. His cat stayed on his chest, purring and keeping a steady vigil, offering love and warmth. I believe it comforted both of them. When my grandfather died, we took extraordinary steps to make sure that his beloved kitty had the best home in the world, because in the end he was everything to my grandpa.

REACHING OUT

I sent an email to my closest friends on the death of Figgy, as I customarily do when something that matters happens. I will not soon forget the responses I received. One from a dear friend especially sticks in my mind. He gave me his sympathies and shared with me the fact that when his cat of many years died, his pain and grief proved more wrenching than the pain he felt when one of his parents died. In a mysterious and surprising way, his cat of many years left an imprint on his adult life and heart, and offered to him unconditionally a comfort, acceptance, love, and companionship that can only be found in the heart of an innocent animal. I think they were both lucky to have found each other.

I am an only child. My mother lives in Oregon; my father in Los Angeles. They divorced when I was four. My father remarried and had three children, which presented me with one stepbrother and two stepsisters. I'm uncomfortable with the word "step," as it denotes a non-relation, a non-connection. I do confess to some occasional estrangement with that part of my family tree, but I would never wish to discount the bloodline that exists between us and the value it represents to our lives. It's true that we did not grow up in the same house with the same parents, but our father is the common denominator, and I would fight anyone who says that we are not the strongest of siblings in the truest sense of the word. We are all our father's children, and there is no "step" in that!

My relationship with my father was not always amicable. It suffered the traumas of divorce, parental control, and mis-judgments on both our sides. He was just a young man of 21 when I was born, and so I tend to think that we did a lot of growing up together. I still laugh at his notion that I was his practice child. It was the truth. As I matured, I learned the value of taking things for what they were versus what I wished or hoped they would be. In that acceptance I gained a relationship with my father that was honest, loving, and real. We speak a few times each month and share stories of love, business, and future hopes. He is one of the most positive and upbeat people I have ever known; an influence, love, and life mentor I treasure.

My relationship with my mother is not all I hoped it would be. She has chosen to distance herself, perhaps as punishment to me because I was unable to give her all the attention she required after the birth and during the raising of my daughter. Because my mother was an only child as well, we were extremely close in my youth. When she failed to be my number one priority, I failed to be hers. The fact that I am not her number one priority matters little to me. She is my mom and I love her. Even though distance and circumstance has changed my family dynamic, I love them completely.

They say you can't choose your family, but I have met many people, myself included, who would beg to differ.

We accept people and animals into our lives and treat them like our family because that is what they become. They are not one centimeter less valuable or important. Along with my parents, aunts, uncles, sisters and brothers, I have found additional non-related members that have become my family. Some walk on two legs, some on four.

Family: it's what we find along the way.

TAMMY-ISM: *Too often we realize what we had in a relationship after it is gone. Not good enough. Family comes in all forms, all sizes, and all species. Be aware. Notice who is standing there beside you offering a hug when it's needed, who gives you a lift when your car breaks down, who is on the other end of the phone night after night listening, and who is forever happy to see you when you come home. I'll stack my so-called dysfunctional friends and my furry critters up against anyone else, anytime. Family equals team. We are a team in each other's lives, and that's pretty much all that matters.*

THE COMEBACK KID

Nobody is stronger, nobody is weaker than someone who came back. There is nothing you can do to such a person because whatever you could do is less than what has already been done. We have already paid the price.

- ELIE WIESEL

S o, ladies, here we are. When all is said and done, we wake up to the realization that we have lived half our lives and find ourselves standing at the gate of mid-life without a husband. If we have learned anything in the process, it would be that happiness does not come in the form of a wedding ring, and happily ever after is always a promise waiting to happen.

Our tires may have worn tread, our windshield may be pitted by life's sandstorms, our upholstery may be in need of a nip and tuck, but make no mistake, ladies, our engines are revving and more than ready to win the race. Classic, stylish, and devilishly cunning, we are in our prime for our comeback. Honey, if you're under 50 years of age, stand back and watch our smoke.

FAKING IT OR MAKING IT?

I want to share a secret with you. This little tidbit of truth saw me through bankruptcy, poverty, unemployment, a job with little promise, and a lackluster daily grind. When the time came to try something I had never done before, but I knew in my heart I could accomplish it, I faked my way through. Women have been faking things for years. Why not this?

No one knows what you are capable or incapable of doing, except you. If you momentarily lack confidence, but you know you have what it takes, fake it. It's in the knowing yourself, of your heart's desires, and the willingness to go out on that limb, that will lead you to where you want to go.

We have seen it time and time again, those days when we didn't think we could hide our misery, sadness, and despair from our children or our friends; those days when it took everything we had to abandon our bathrobes and pretend that life was as it should be. We have all been there. We have faked it. If you give it some thought, you might realize that it was the faking it that often brought you back to where you needed to be.

We have gone to work when we were certain we would have a mental breakdown. We have gotten all gussied up in a smart outfit, put on lipstick, and styled our hair when we were convinced that what looked back at us in the mirror's reflection was utterly unattractive. We faked it.

When we have been called upon by our children or our employers to perform a job we had never done before, we smiled with confidence, all the while fearing that they would see right through us. Nine times out of ten, we have raised the bar in what we have been able to accomplish. We might have faked it in the beginning, but the proof is always in the pudding; we have delivered. Doing things people don't expect of us isn't unusual. Succeeding at those things is also very customary. Why, then, do we continue to doubt ourselves?

Our mind-set is often pigeonholed in the rigid confines of our present world, reminding us of our limitations and allowing us to use the word "can't" far too often. To hell with that! If you have to temporarily fake it to find your way back to you, you are simply using a tool that was given you. Use it without apology.

If we dress and act the part of what it is we want or need to be, we can become it. We then find ourselves thinking the dream, talking the thought, and in the end, walking the talk. It happens every day. It's time we recognized that what we may have perceived as an extraordinary ability to conceal our shortcomings is, in fact, one of our greatest survival skills.

Faking it is our way of taking ourselves to that point where we are allowed to become what we want ourselves to be. Both personally and professionally, the ability to fake it is a viable tool.

Throughout my life I was aware that I was capable of managing certain jobs and tasks for which I had no training. What I lacked in experience, I made up for with willingness and attitude. Before I share with you what I have been able to accomplish through this method, I also want to make it very clear, that I, probably like yourself, have not always lived in a rose garden.

I lost a home in foreclosure, went bankrupt, was unemployed, had my utilities shut off, suffered bad credit, suffered two miscarriages and had mounds of health care bills. Last but not least, at one point I was on food stamps. Now, let's talk about what I was able to make happen despite life's hardships and obstacles.

I started a property management company with absolutely no experience. The business provided me with an excellent income, vital contacts, and knowledge I would need and use for years to come. I provided excellent service, knowledge, and was known in the field as a commendable source. I owned the company for almost ten years. I faked it.

I started a television production company and deemed myself producer with absolutely no experience in the field. I owned the company for four years and sold the business at a sizeable profit. If anyone in the city wanted their project filmed and aired, I was usually their first call. I faked it.

I started a company specializing in survival training and supplies with absolutely no experience. I booked public speaking engagements, was a guest on local television and radio networks, and became the authority on preparedness for the Los Angeles area. The business lasted 13 years, and placed me at the top of the list as a source to media and local agencies. I received commendations for my contributions from the City of Los Angeles as well as local agencies. I faked it.

I was contracted to host a radio talk show in Los Angeles, fielding live on-air callers and booking guests for weekly topic discussions, and I did it with no previous experience in the field. I faked it.

I became the spokesperson for the mature, single woman, penned a book that alerted women in similar life circumstances to the joyful realities of the single life, and conduct lectures, seminars, and workshops for mature, single women everywhere. Here is the clincher. I didn't have to fake anything. The irony is not lost on me that much of my past experience was garnered through my ability to fake my way through. This most recent career was started in my early fifties, and I doubt it will be my last effort.

It would be an injustice if I allowed you to believe that every venture I tried was a success. I have had my share of crash-and-burn experiences, three that remain vivid in my mind. Suffering the embarrassment of failure is a bruising experience. I learned how to lose gracefully, but I never felt the urge to learn to like it. As years passed, I realized that I had learned much from my failed attempts. The knowledge and sting of those experiences led me to the understanding and acceptance of the fact that if you risk nothing, you gain less.

What is my secret, you ask? No secret. I decided early in life that I was going to be the only one who set my limitations. I skirted around the formalities and cut to the chase. Am I advising you to misrepresent yourselves? No. I'm asking you to be the one who defines you. If you know you can, you can. If you don't do what you know you can do, you've lost. And if these pages have spoken anything to you, it is that your life is not about compromise or losing. It's about winning. Failure is not an option, simply because the only failure that truly exists is in not trying.

When we talk about our personal lives, the same rules do not apply. Faking happiness only buys us a world of hurt. It is the opposite end of the spectrum that must be faced and embraced when we deal with our family, our future, and ourselves. The faking of your everyday attempts to get by, get ahead, and make things happen will inevitably work to your benefit. But we should never fake happiness and fulfillment. That could easily turn into a life sentence of misery.

So many opportunities are offered to us in the course of our lives. We often don't recognize them for what they are. Unfortunately, when we do recognize opportunity, we often look the other way. Distracted by our lives in motion or our fear to see what we could be, we miss out on some of the best gifts life has to offer. Using our keen awareness of what we believe to be our shortcomings, our faults, and our inabilities, we excuse ourselves from the challenges of seizing the moments that could define us. Instead, we cling to our perceived inadequacies and protect our excuses from exposure. In doing so, we forget the most simple of our awareness; we are capable.

Filled with our own hopes, dreams, strengths, and promises, we possess the means to live happily after divorce. Growing older is not an option; it is a gift. It is our job, ladies, to take that gift, open it, and run like hell with it. This is your time for renewal, discovery, dreams, and celebration. This moment in your life is fleeting. Pay attention.

Whatever path you choose to take, whatever choices you make along the way, know that you have my personal prayer and belief that you will make it to wherever it is you want to go. Travel light. You will need to pack your courage, your forgiveness, your patience and determination, and your creativity. Leave behind your hate, resentment, blame, and guilt; they will slow your journey and weigh down your flight. You are the hope and the life of your future. You are your own promise. Without having taken your hand, without having heard your story, I know you. I **am** you. And I'm behind you all the way.

TAMMY-ISM: *When I lectured on surviving disasters in the eighties and nineties, I talked about the "flee or fight" syndrome. It is a basic animal instinct, a decision made in a split second to either fight the foe you face or run like hell. The foes faced by the mature woman can be many, but few are more formidable than her own self. Once you get out of your own way, once you cease making excuses, once you make up your mind that you will be happy, it will happen.*

Have faith in yourself. You were not brought into this world to be unhappy, unfulfilled, unchallenged. Do not settle. Whatever you choose to do with your life, do it with all your heart and breath. This is your chance, possibly your last chance. Make it happen.

Sources/References

AARP. 2006. Foundation Women's Leadership Circle Study, The Looking at Act II of Women's Lives; Thriving & Striving from 45 On. http://assets.aarp.org/rgcenter/general/wicresearch.pdf.

AARP. 2004. Sexuality at Midlife & Beyond. Study Update of Attitudes & Behaviors. Conducted by TNS NFO, Atlanta. http://aarp.org/rgcenter/general/2004_sexuality.pdf.

AARP. May 2004. The Divorce Experience. A Study at Midlife and Beyond/Executive Summary. Report conducted by Knowledge Networks, Inc. Report by Xenia P. Montenegro, PhD. http://assets.aarp.org/rgcenter/general/divorce.pdf.

AARP. 2003. Lifestyles, Dating & Romance, A Study of Midlife Singles/Research Report. http://assets.aarp.org/ rgcenter/general/singles.pdf.

Bleck, Tammy. A Survey, The Wants and Needs of The Single Woman Past 50. Tammy Talks, LLC. July 2005. www.TammyBleck.com.

Chadwick, Bruce A. and Heaton, Tim B., eds. 1999. Statistical *Handbook on the American Family, 2d ed.* Phoenix, AZ: Oryx Press.

Gibbs, Nancy. 2005. Midlife Crisis? Bring it On! *Time Magazine,* May 16, 2005.

Hales, Dianne. 2004. Getting Yourself Back on Track. *Parade Magazine*, March 28, 2004.

Kuczynski, Alex. 2004. Till Death Do Us … *New York Times.* Reprinted in *The Gazette* (Colorado Springs, CO), August 23, 2004.

Mahoney, Sarah. 2003. Seeking Love. *AARP The Magazine*, November/December 2003, http://assets.aarp.org/rgcenter /general/singles_1.pdf

Sheehy, Gail. 2006. The New Seasoned Woman. *Parade Magazine*, January 8, 2006.

Sheehy, Gail. 2005. Life Begins at 60. *Parade Magazine*, December 11, 2005.

Smart Marriages. The Coalition for Marriage, Family & Couples Education. http://www.smartmarriages.com/index.html

Unmarried America. Female Friendships Have a Positive Effect on Health; May 22, 2005. http://www.unmarried america.org/members/news/2005/may-news/female_ friendships-have-positive-effect-on-health.htr

U.S. Bureau of the Census. 2001. Statistical Abstract of the United States, 2001: The National Data Book. 121st edition. Prepared by Commerce Department Economic and Statistics Administration, Bureau of the Census, Washington, D.C.

Yanek, Dawn. 2007. Are You Better Off Single? MSN News. February 2007. http://msn.match.com/msn/ article.aspx?articleid=6320&menuid=7&lid419

About the Author

◆➤ **TAMMY BLECK** was born and raised in Los Angeles, California, and spent the first 40 years of her life calling L.A. her home. Born far from privilege, Tammy worked her way towards success but not without experiencing the harsh realities of life. After brief stints in the corporate sector, Tammy joined the ranks of the self employed. She has since embarked on six separate careers, varying from radio talk show host and public speaker to survival preparedness expert. She has been featured on ABC, NBC, and CBS affiliates, The Daily News and the Los Angeles Times, as well as countless other networks and publications.

Tammy was married to her high school sweetheart for 25 years, has been single for the past five years, and is 54 years young. Her in-depth survey of 100 single women between the ages of 50 and 69 revealed such astonishing results that she was compelled to write a book about it. Yet another career was launched!

Ms. Bleck travels nationwide providing key note presentations, seminars, workshops and consulting services. Tammy's amazing ability to touch the hearts of her audiences with her experience, wit and wisdom has made her a popular choice on the speaking circuit.

Tammy resides in Denver, Colorado with her dog Maddy, and her cat Henry. She spends her spare time with her daughter, Amanda, who attends college in Denver. Her hobbies include needlepoint, antique shopping, walking with her dog, perusing bookstores and socializing with her friends.

Book Bonus Offer!

◆◆ **AS A SPECIAL THANK YOU** for purchasing *Single Past 50…Now What?* you will receive a bonus of amazing value catering to the needs, wants and interests of the single woman.

A fabulous rolodex of over 100 web sites that will educate, inform and support you as you venture through life as the marvelous single woman that you are. Whether you need help with starting your own business, want to access travel options, have finance concerns, health and fitness issues, support groups; it's all here. And it's all exclusively yours….**FREE.**

Ready to claim your free gift?
Go to **www.tammybleck.com/bookbonus**
Get yours today!

The
Nowhere Novel
&
18 Other Short
and
Shorter Stories

For Those Who Like Stories with Complex
Characters and Unexpected Outcomes.

DAVID L. ROBINSON

authorHOUSE®

AuthorHouse™
1663 Liberty Drive
Bloomington, IN 47403
www.authorhouse.com
Phone: 1 (800) 839-8640

Published by AuthorHouse 07/25/2018

ISBN: 978-1-5462-5135-4 (sc)
ISBN: 978-1-5462-5134-7 (e)

Library of Congress Control Number: 2018908301

Print information available on the last page.

Contents

To Lynn, Mom, and Dad

(With special thanks to Jerry Bumpus and Elizabeth Chater)

The Nowhere Novel

Chapter 1

Frank Darnell glanced over the laptop to see if his co-author, Austin Rice Jr., was making any progress on the ninth chapter of their novel.

It appeared that Austin had reached another "slow spot," his euphemism for his frequent writing blocks. His eyes were closed, and he was humming, a recently developed habit Austin said calmed him but irritated the hell out of Frank.

"How are you doing?" Frank asked, anticipating the answer.

Austin looked up; rubbing the sweat from his forehead.

"Slow as molasses. Running into some character development problems."

"That seems to be a trend."

"And the sarcasm is supposed to be helpful?"

"More of a reality check."

It was their second weekend retreat at the Seaside Cottage in San Diego, and Frank had promised it would be his last, even if Austin continued to badger him about the past.

"Maybe we need a break," Austin suggested.

Frank shook his head. "We've only been writing for a couple of hours."

"But I think we're getting back into our rhythm.

Sometimes, it takes a bit of face-to-face writing to get up to speed."

"Right."

Frank checked the work log he had started after their first meeting. As he had told Austin then, without tracking their progress, they'd never finish the book. There was an entry for each phone call, e-mail discussion, and Skype meeting dating back to the original plot outline they had scribbled on a cocktail napkin.

They had got off to a good start, enthusiastic about the story—a 60s-era mystery thriller based on the real-life murder of a prominent attorney. They had agreed to write regularly, have monthly check-ins, and meet every Labor Day weekend at the Seaside Cottage Resort. Frank took the Amtrak Coaster from Oakland, and Austin drove from his home in Phoenix. They would write for two days and return home to continue developing their assigned chapters.

Frank's latest update explained that they had completed the first eight chapters; also, that Austin had become obsessed with titles. They had initially thought that 'The American Criminal' was a good working title, but then Austin had said that he preferred 'The Great American Crime.' "I think having 'The Great American' in the title is a plus," he said. Frank had insisted that they shouldn't be concerned with titles, but Austin would regularly e-mail new ideas. In the last month, they had managed to finish outlines of another two chapters.

During their most recent Skype discussion, they had talked about the merits of first making it into an e-book, although Austin hadn't been sure. Frank also had expressed his concerns that they weren't making sufficient progress and said that he was planning a hiatus from the project. Austin had insisted they should "press on," once again reminding Frank of "the big secret and your promise."

Austin pushed his I-pad aside and said, "You know, we never said it was going to be easy."

"True, but it wasn't supposed to be nearly impossible, either. It seems we've established a painful process of four steps forward and three steps back."

Austin frowned. "I suppose I'm the one who takes us backward?"

"Didn't say that. But after nearly two years, we should have had this thing done."

"Other writing partners have been able to write a book."

"They probably have more synergy, a commitment to making it happen in a reasonable time frame and one that is based on mutual respect."

"We've had respect."

"Along with mistrust, coercion, and frustration. I accept that I'm an asshole for initially letting you intimidate me over that thing."

"That's overblown hyperbole." Austin began pacing around the room, humming softly. He stopped to examine the faux Monet painting.

"I'm going to take a short walk on the beach. Clear my head. Come back and get chapter nine in order."

Frank laughed.

"Fine, but Austin we must talk about this. I want out. I've thought long and hard about it and am serious about what we discussed earlier. You can continue working on the book and have all rights to what we've done so far."

Austin folded his arms.

"That's a topic for later discussion. Remember."

"You've made it hard to forget."

"One more trip here and we'll probably get it done."

"That's bullshit. We should have called it the Nowhere Novel. It will never get done. I don't want to spend another damn weekend here."

"Whatever," Austin said smiling. "I'll be back soon."

Chapter 2

Frank looked out the window, waiting to see Austin walk along the beach. Several people were sitting under umbrellas, but he didn't find Austin.

"Probably never made it out of the hotel."

He opened Austin's laptop and saw the notation: "Chapter 9—Austin's Input," but there was only one sentence. His notepad had a series of doodles and indecipherable notes.

"Great. Can't write more than a few sentences at a time. What's he thinking?"

Frank had learned a great deal about Austin's thought process and overall approach, including his penchant for starting in the middle of a chapter and then returning to the open and close. As he told Susan before leaving home that morning, "Austin is a good sportswriter...period. He doesn't have the imagination nor the discipline to write fiction."

Frank wrote a few more sentences and then switched files to work on his own book. His editor was pushing him to finish the initial draft, and Frank felt anxious about the impending deadlines. He had started *The Disappearing Novel* only three months earlier after much discussion with

Susan and his editor, who had suggested the basic plotline. Two college acquaintances decide to write a novel together and meet on a yearly basis to write and review their progress. "It explores long-standing grudges, jealousy, and the secret that one of them uses to continue the joint authorship," the editor had explained. Frank had initially balked at the premise, arguing that it "is way too autobiographical and risks a lawsuit because Austin will be extremely pissed." Frank only agreed after much discussion on how the plot could be appropriately "neutralized" to avoid conflict with Austin and the editor's insistence that legal action was unlikely. He still agonized over how to obscure the characters and make Austin a sympathetic character—or at least not overly obnoxious.

He did feel guilty. Even though he knew that Austin wasn't capable of finishing his portion of their novel, Frank felt bad about abandoning him and didn't like the deception involved in writing a different book. There was also the residual guilt over "the incident" about which his co-author enjoyed reminding him and anger that he had let himself become ensnared in Austin's plot. That was why he had to break it off before the end of this trip.

Frank saw a new e-mail from Susan. He was late sending her an update. "I hope all goes well there," she wrote. "Taking John to his baseball game. Have you told Austin yet? Please put an end to it, before we face even more grief."

Susan understood his rationale for continuing to meet with Austin, but after their "clearing the air" discussion two months earlier, she had been urging him to stop.

"Tell John to have a great game," he wrote. "I have repeated my plan to quit the book. Of course, he's not enthusiastic about it. I imagine we'll have a rather uncomfortable showdown later today or tomorrow. See you soon. Promise. Meanwhile, back to the real story."

Frank continued to work on *The Disappearing Novel*. His editor had asked for a status report on Monday.

Chapter 3

When Austin returned to the room two hours later, Frank could smell the alcohol.

"You've been in the bar, haven't you?"

"Just a quick stop after my invigorating beach walk. Ready to get back to the writing. I've got some new ideas."

Austin slumped in his chair and turned his laptop on. Frank watched as Austin resumed his agonizingly slow typing.

"Austin, we need to continue our talk about the future. I told Susan that I've made my last trip."

Austin started humming again.

"I'd say another year at the most, and we're done. But I think you'll agree that it's not a good idea to walk away at this point."

"You know Austin, the sad thing about this collaboration is that it is based on a drunken night, an initially creative idea, and then your threat, coupled with my insecurity and inability to resolve the situation earlier."

"That seems a bit harsh."

"Is what it is. And why the need to write this thing anyway? You've got a good writing job and have a great family."

"You're mocking me."

"Of course not."

"Knowing that I've always wanted to write a novel and that we had this big idea."

"That has morphed from a decent concept to a hodgepodge of different directions."

"That's part of the creative process."

"And again, you know that part of what has kept me going this last year was your not-so-subtle threats and my inertia…the inability to put a stop to it."

"Let's not dwell on that. Besides, I really wasn't threatening you about that evening, just reminding you I was a witness. I haven't said much about it for a long time. So, let's concentrate on getting the book done. I'm sure we can, over the next year."

"No, we can't and won't. Why is this so important to you? And why am I so essential to the process? We're not really friends anymore, just two guys linked by this book. Our original intentions were reasonable; the basic premise was sound. But over the last year, it's become clear that it isn't working. We have two different styles that just aren't meshing. And besides…"

"You always did resent me, didn't you?" said Austin. "Even back in college."

"How's that?"

Austin was no longer smiling. "I was generally more popular with the girls, and I was on the football team. You were a semester behind me and always seemed to be looking for guidance or support. I sensed that there was jealousy on your part."

Frank leaned forward. "I don't remember it that way,

Austin. We were certainly different, but we both had our strengths and weaknesses."

"I always looked out for you."

"Well, I tried to do the same for you. I recall several occasions when I backed you up. Besides, I think you've become a bit jealous. You know I've had some success as an author, and I think you envy that."

"Don't turn it back on me."

Frank stood. "I'm not trying to turn it back on you. Look, Austin. I'm sorry for my part in all of this. The original sin, the agreement to write the book based on our supposed friendship—and most of all, letting it get this far. I accept the responsibility. But it's not working. I'm not doing my best work. You're not happy here. I know you enjoy telling people that you're working on a novel. But based on my experience writing two relatively successful books, I know that publishers won't buy it."

Austin clapped his hands. "Stop it," he said. "Enough of the negativity. Quiet. I need to think."

He covered his eyes and began rocking back and forth. "I'm done for the day," he said. "I'll cancel our reservation and eat in my room tonight."

"Fine. Suits me."

Chapter 4

They were now working at opposite sides of the room, Frank at the table and Austin on the couch closest to the window. Frank's suitcase leaned against the door.

Before Austin had arrived, Frank e-mailed Susan,

"I'm walking on eggshells again. This time, it's even more uncomfortable because of yesterday's argument."

Frank was now concentrating on his book, having already packed the other manuscript for Austin. He glanced up and saw that Austin was watching him.

"Austin, I've organized my material so that you should be able to connect everything on your own. I'll be glad to share my agent contacts."

"I just need a little more time. Look, I didn't tell you yesterday, but I've lost my job, and I need this to work."

"I'm sorry to hear that, Austin, but I still can't work with you any longer."

As he walked to the window, Frank could hear Austin whisper. "You don't want me to push it, do you?"

"Sorry?"

"Frank, I didn't want to say anything, and I do regret acting like a jerk about this, but lately, our secret seems to be the glue holding this together."

"What? Your lame threats ensured that we would work together as friendly writing partners so that we could publish a book?" Frank shouted. "There's nothing left to say. I've already told Susan. I explained what happened. It's done."

Austin laughed.

"I don't believe you. You never had the balls to be that confrontational."

"It wasn't easy. But I did tell her."

"Whatever; but I doubt you gave her all the details. Anyway, I'd like us to overlook that part of our relationship so we can finish the book and then move on."

"Austin, you opened the door on this. So, I confessed the huge mistake—that I slept with her bridesmaid two nights before our wedding. Sure, she was upset…but we worked through it."

Frank was short of breath and his heart was racing; the same reaction he had whenever Austin had hinted at "the secret" or "the incident."

Austin closed his eyes. "I still don't believe you. Otherwise, you wouldn't be here."

Frank pushed his laptop aside. "It certainly has been a strange situation. I originally came here before because I thought the book could work and did want to help you. Your promise to tell Susan about that night was an initial but, surprisingly, a minor motivation--as I said, partially based on my profound guilt, as if I needed to be punished. That's all my problem. If you had worked a little harder, we might have finished the book. But I came here this weekend to tell you in person that it's over and we should move on. I was going to call or e-mail with my decision, but Susan convinced me to meet with you."

"I didn't think you'd be a quitter."

"Not quitting; just moving on. Besides, you don't even have the facts right."

Austin shook his head. "What do you mean?"

Frank hadn't intended to say anything more, knowing how angry Austin would become.

"You think I slept with Marcy Palmer that night, don't you?"

"That's who I saw you with in the hallway outside our rooms."

"Yes, I was talking with her before I met up with another woman. But Marcy was never in my room."

"Okay, I give up. If not Marcy, then who? I know you were with someone, by the way you looked."

"Forget it."

Austin stood and moved closer to Frank. "I'll call your bluff. Finish your short story."

"You're right. I was with a woman, but not who you think."

"The suspense is killing me…who was it?"

Frank knew he should stop. *Just let it go*, he thought. But Austin's smug grin was irritating.

"Really want me to say?"

"Obviously."

Frank watched Austin's blank expression. *He doesn't have any idea.*

"It was Sally, your wife of the last five years."

Austin didn't hear anything after the first three words.

"You bastard," he shouted. "So, rather than tell the truth, you bring my wife into it? What a feeble way of accepting responsibility. She would never do that with you. No way."

"Remember that we had gone out before you two started dating?"

"So what? She had moved on and was no longer interested in you."

"Normally not. But you broke up for a few days, she and I were both drunk, and yes, I was a huge jerk."

"Now you're pissing me off. This is pretty low, even for you."

"Look Austin, you've forced this. I would never have said anything. If it's any consolation, the evening meant nothing, and we never got together again."

As Austin lunged forward to grab at Frank, he tripped over his briefcase and fell. Frank extended his right hand, but Austin pulled away.

"Son of a bitch."

"Austin, I'm sorry, I didn't want to go this far."

Austin slowly got up. "I still don't believe you. But I'm going to take a walk and clear my head."

"Fine, but I won't be here when you get back. I'm checking out."

Austin's voice was now high pitched and whiny. "I'm still not convinced that you have told Susan everything. Even if you did, you probably wouldn't want me calling her to rehash the messy situation. I know how sensitive she can be. And, as much as I hate you for what you've just said, I still want to get the book done—and then we're finished. We'll be friends no more. I'll send you details on our next meeting and will work doubly hard to get my chapters to you."

Chapter 5

The following Labor Day, Austin arrived at the Seaside Cottage earlier than usual. He was in an unusually cheerful mood.

He clapped his hands. "I've got a great intro to chapter 14."

They had been writing since early that morning.

"What is it?"

"It starts with the reporter finding a note that suggests the real murderer might be the original suspect's cousin."

"That seems like a good approach. Have you fleshed out the rest of the earlier chapter? Seems to be one of the problems that you get started on a specific chapter and can't get through."

Austin leaned back and smiled, ignoring the unwelcome critique. "It's a give-and-take process," he said.

"I can see that you are making notes, but we have to go faster."

They wrote for several more hours without talking to each other.

"I'm feeling confident about this," Austin finally announced.

"Hope so. Remember that you said you'd have your chapters ready."

"Right. I'm almost on schedule."

"Austin, I want to help you on this, but as I said earlier, I can only commit to a few more months. If we can't get it done by then, I have to move on."

Austin began to hum and then said, "We probably will get it done this year. But if not, I think you'll want to keep going until it's finished. Besides, Sharon, you did make that promise."

She closed her laptop and stood. "It wasn't actually a promise if you recall. I offered to help as a semi-friend, but I have other projects I need to complete as well."

"Whatever. Let's take a break."

"Fine, I think I'll go for a short walk."

"I'll stay here."

After she left, Austin continued writing for a few minutes and then walked to the picture window. He saw Sharon Johnson, an English professor at Phoenix University, stop to talk to a few people gathered along the boardwalk. She looked up in his direction. He nodded.

"Another year like this one, and our great American novel will be in bookstores," he said. "Just like I always thought it would be."

The Reluctant Laughingstock

Joe Rollins leaned back in the shrink-wrapped recliner and listened to the latest addition to his collection of laughs, the one he had recorded earlier that evening at the Cool Ray Condo Complex's annual "Get Reacquainted" party. Joe replayed the tape several times to confirm it was a new variety—a wheezing, hiccupping, out-of-control chortle. He labeled the cassette and placed it in a worn leather case.

"That's one for the ages," Joe said, the same comment he made when adding each laugh to his "Compendium of Random and Exuberant Laughter."

Joe had begun collecting laughs two years earlier, just before his mother died; it was also about the time that he had had his automobile accident in Houston and made the subsequent move to Los Angeles. He started taping them only after researching how other "laugh anthropologists" had approached the subject, carefully analyzing his motivation, and receiving a gentle admonishment from his brother. "It's fine if you are truly interested in this ha-ha business," Henry told him. "On the other hand, if you're just trying to get back at the old man, you're going in the wrong direction."

Joe initially doubted that the collection would amount to much, but he continued recording the laughs because of the cathartic relief it provided and the positive response he received from the laughing community, whose members also called themselves "mirth enthusiasts." He already had cataloged more than 60 different types—including the scared-nervous laugh, the full-throated screamer that seemed to frighten some people, and the belly-influx howler (which he claimed to have discovered)—and cross-referenced them by sex, ethnicity, and region. Joe hadn't planned on setting a record, but according to the latest Guinness Book, he was now listed after the entry for the Most People Laughing at One Time. Joe also had been invited to speak at this year's International Laugh Symposium in Cleveland. In anticipation of the supposedly prestigious event, he lost 40 pounds from a dreary cabbage and melon diet, replaced his bifocals with light green contact lenses, and purchased a darker hairpiece that would complement his pale complexion.

Joe knew that most people considered the laugh collection to be peculiar. At that evening's party, one of his neighbors, a heavily tattooed man who wore a diamond stud earring and talked like a pirate ("Arr Arr, good grog indeed," he told the irritated hostess) asked him about the recordings and then shook his head. "It's beyond odd; you've sailed into some strange waters, mate. But whatever gives you the grand pleasures is okay by me. Arr."

Later, an older woman with a floppy canvas hat covering her tangle of white hair stared at Joe for a few seconds and whispered, "What for and how do you do it?" Joe started to explain, but she interrupted, insisting "Maybe it's an interesting hobby. I knit socks and hats."

Joe considered the party's highlight to be discovering an understated laugh from Francine, the young woman in

Apartment 3-K. They had spoken a few times in the lobby, and Joe thought she was special, more reserved than some of the other Cool Ray Condo women he found to be brash and intimidating. However, Francine's laugh wasn't very cheery. *She sounded tired or irritated about something,* he thought. *She was probably in a foul mood and let it affect her laugh.* Joe wasn't sure if Francine even knew he was recording the laughs at the party. Not everyone did.

After making a few notes about the party in his laugh journal, Joe turned off the lights and went to bed. He rarely watched TV anymore, except when The Tonight Show's guests were comedians, affording him a chance to analyze the audiences' laughs. There were always a few standouts that were more distinct than the others. There was no time for that now; he had to get up early. His supervisor had scheduled a major audit.

—•◆•—

Joe figured that he probably hadn't heard his first laugh until he was about five years old. Random laughter was frowned upon in their house. Unlike their neighbors' homes that had signs reading "Our Happy Home" or "Families Live, Love, and Laugh Together," his father had nailed a wooden placard over the fireplace that advised: "Life Is No Laughing Matter." As Joe later learned, Sam Rollins firmly believed that he had endured more than his share of frustration in a glass-half-empty life and saw no reason for merriment. He decided that his wife and two sons should behave likewise. Joe recalled being a toddler and making faces that would elicit laughter from most parents but only earned a solemn expression from his father and his mother's tight smile.

His first close-up exposure to laughter occurred at a friend's house when the family was watching a TV variety show, and everyone laughed heartily. Joe was surprised at the spontaneous outburst and wasn't sure how to respond. His laugh was so muffled that no one paid attention.

He later became more accustomed to laughter during school recesses when the other boys and girls would play and tease each other. Joe still didn't feel comfortable laughing in front of them. They eventually decided he was either too shy or just didn't like their funny behavior. At an early age, he acquired the nickname "Jolly Joe;" later learning it was a derisive moniker. When Joe tried to explain his concern at not feeling free to laugh, his father said simply, "As you boys will learn, there are many more important things in life than idle laughter."

—•◆•—

As usual, Joe was up the next day by 5 a.m. His morning routine rarely varied: shower; get dressed; have a staple breakfast of coffee, toast, and three prunes; and then take a short bus ride to work. He rarely talked to anyone, preferring instead to listen to the passengers' muted conversations. The only significant event occurred when a young man with Tourette's syndrome shouted loud references to female genitalia, and his elderly seatmate cried "Pipe down, pipsqueak."

Joe's work day was the usual rush of tedious calculations, and report filing and sorting. His primary responsibility was to process the insurance claimants' payment requests; a job made more difficult as Mr. Stufflebeam's list of "precautionary checks and balances" increased.

He spent his half-hour lunch break reviewing the

Readers Digest humor columns, which activity he briefly interrupted to audition the laughs of two other clerks who stopped by. Baxter tried to engage him in one of his rants about the country's economic malaise, but Joe managed to avoid his rambling speech. He shook his head. "Gotta check on the new filing system," Joe said, leaving Baxter alone at the lunchroom table.

Upon arriving home that evening, Joe instantly knew that something was wrong. The first thing he always did on entering the cramped apartment was to look directly at the oak stand. The Compendium wasn't there. A small glass vase with a single red rose stood in its place.

"My God," he said.

Joe quickly glanced around the front room to be sure he hadn't overlooked the case. Nothing else seemed out of place. "Why would anyone take it? Maybe someone noticed." He ran into the hallway and began knocking on his neighbors' doors.

"Have you seen anything unusual today?" he asked Mrs. Harkenstadt. "Looks like someone has entered my apartment and taken a few things. Perhaps you've been aware of strangers walking about?"

She stared through the narrow opening in her doorway and said nervously, "We have a safe place here. The thought of thieves wandering about makes me positively shudder. I haven't seen a soul what doesn't belong here."

He tapped on the door of Apartment 4C and heard a muffled shout. The door opened wide to reveal the pudgy pirate man who wore a multi-colored vest and a paisley bandana that covered the top of his head. "Haven't seen any unknown characters loitering in the vicinity," he responded to Joe's question. "They would know better than to be tampering with my belongings, that's for certain. But I'll keep my one good eye out for you mate."

Joe asked several more neighbors, but all insisted they hadn't seen any strangers or his Compendium. The building manager promised to watch for it but suggested that Joe take another look in his apartment. "I often misplace things," Mr. Crumplin said.

He did search the rooms again, even looking behind the couch and on top of the bookcase, but the collection wasn't there. Joe called the police department to report the theft, and an officious receptionist said it would be a few days before an officer could take a formal report. "We have a system in place," she said. "You can wait for one of our officers to come there or stop by the station and fill out the paperwork."

When he called Henry to cancel their weekly dinner, his brother said, "Maybe this is a sign that you should get a different hobby. Plus, are you ever going to share the story behind it all? Maybe they will understand then. Especially about the goodbye laugh."

—•◆•—

Once he left home to attend college, Joe began researching and experimenting with laughter. At first, he laughed too loudly and at inopportune times—such as before the punch line of a classmate's joke. He began to listen more carefully to the way others laughed.

In his sophomore year, Joe took a popular elective course called the Mechanics of a Laugh, taught by a local comedian who explained the various types and nuances of laughter. He enjoyed the class immensely, but his father found out about it and threatened to reduce the amount of his paltry quarterly allowance. On his next visit home, Joe tried to explain that laughter was healthy and that his desire to learn about it didn't mean he was unmindful of life's challenges or didn't respect his father's values. However, Sam said he was more disappointed in himself for not doing a better job of keeping Joe from wasting his "college career" and preparing him for a life "dedicated to the seriousness of the challenges that await you." Joe's mother reminded him that Sam had "inherited" the stern demeanor from his parents, who had apparently endured their own harsh life experiences. Joe decided to avoid discussing the subject of laughter on his future visits.

—•◆•—

During the next few days, Joe continued searching for the Compendium. One morning, he heard laughter while walking to the elevator and briefly thought it might be one of the tenants listening to his stolen laugh collection. *That's ridiculous; I can't imagine anyone here doing that.*

Joe even took the recorder during a few errands, thinking that he might find a few laughs. However, the thought of starting a new collection was too daunting, and he gave up. *I could never get to the same level again; it just takes too much time and energy.*

A week after the Compendium was stolen, Joe's search was over. Returning home from work late one evening, he found the case leaning against his front door. He rushed inside, sat in the recliner, and began playing the first tape. He heard the same familiar sounds until there was a brief gap. One of the laughs had been erased. Joe frowned. *It makes no sense. Why would someone delete a laugh and then return the case?*

As Joe rechecked the laughs, he heard a light knock on the door. He opened it and saw Francine, who was holding a cassette tape in her left hand. "I'm sorry for taking your collection," she said nervously. "I was careful to remove just my laugh. Still, I should have been more forthright and not made you wonder."

Joe took a step back. "But why?"

"You'll think it odd."

"No. Well perhaps, but tell me anyway."

She was prettier than he recalled. Her light brown hair was pulled back. She had smooth skin and green eyes.

"The laugh didn't represent the way I am. I remember being in a bad place that day and my laugh was harsh, strident, not really me."

"But no one knew it was you."

"You did though."

"That was important?"

"I don't know; yes, I guess so. At first, it didn't bother me. But then every day I seemed to be more upset, knowing that I was being misrepresented. At least, thinking that I was."

It was the first time he had seen her smile.

"How did you get in?"

"I followed your cleaning lady. I told her I was leaving you a present, which I did."

"The rose."

"Yes."

Joe opened the door wider. "Please, I didn't mean to

keep you standing out there. Would you like to come in for a cup of coffee or something?"

Francine stepped into the room and then stopped. "Another time. I've got to get back to my…my feet."

"Your what?"

"I collect rabbit's feet."

"Rabbit's feet?"

"Strange, isn't it? I started as a young girl when my father brought one back from a sales meeting. It grew from there."

"I don't consider it that odd."

"Well, some certainly do. Ask three people, and two will usually say it's quite weird. But the reason I collect them is simple. It was something I could share with him. It brought us even closer." She paused, watching Joe organize the tapes. "Mind if I ask how you got started gathering the laughter?"

—•◆•—

The goodbye laugh Henry referred to in a prior phone conversation happened at their father's funeral. Sam's will specified that he didn't want a memorial or "any other assemblage of relatives, one-time acquaintances and other strangers telling asinine anecdotes." However, Helen was so befuddled at her husband's sudden death that she allowed a gathering of friends to meet at the Odd Fellows temple, and somehow, it turned into a formal funeral.

Toward the end of the somber ceremony, guests were invited to come close to the open casket and say goodbye to Sam. Joe initially was hesitant to do so, but Henry somehow persuaded him that "Later, you'll be glad you took a last look." They stood close and looked down at Sam, whose face was painted with pancake makeup and rouge. While he couldn't be certain, Joe thought his father was smiling. Joe began laughing, softly at first but then in a high-pitched volume he couldn't control. Several people waved at him to be quiet, but Joe's unrestrained laughter echoed throughout the stuffy auditorium. Henry and their uncle finally escorted Joe to the back of the hall where he remained until the last Odd Fellow had left.

—•◆•—

Joe was still perplexed that Francine had taken the Compendium. As she waited in the entryway, he wondered if she would understand. *It's the first time I've ever said much of anything.* "You know, I've never told anyone how it all started," he said quietly. "My brother calls it a big secret, and it is more complicated than your reason for collecting rabbits' feet. I'll give you the short version. But please sit."

Explaining the family's laughter moratorium and his gradual interest in "the how and why of laughing," Joe sensed he might be boring her with too much detail. He watched carefully to see if she was alarmed about his funeral faux pau. Francine smiled but was otherwise non-committal. *At least she didn't make a face.*

"My final act of rebellion was establishing a modest comedy store scholarship in my father's name," he continued. "But he got the last guffaw. Even though he didn't have a huge estate and most went to my mother, he did leave my brother $500, and I got his collection of Living a Serious Life books and the Life Is No Laughing Matter plaque that hung in our house. During the last few years, I have made peace with his unhappiness and aversion to laughter. He just wasn't a happy person, and it made him uncomfortable when others found the humor in life. I've since made my collection a true hobby rather than an act of defiance. That's my story."

He leaned back on the couch. *Maybe it makes sense to her.*

"I understand your motivation better now," she said. "I hope you don't think I was too snoopy."

"No, I guess I feel better finally saying something."

Francine stood. "Well, I should be getting back. Meanwhile, listen to the laugh. I hope you'll agree that it's better, more like I am. It's not fake. I was watching an old I Love Lucy episode where she is working on the candy making assembly line, and I started laughing so hard. Then I pulled out my recorder. Of course, if you want I'll laugh right into yours."

"No, that's not necessary. I'll take a listen. And thanks for coming by. I do think we should get together sometime."

She started to leave, then turned back to face Joe.

"You did know, didn't you?"

Joe stepped closer. "Know what?"

"Never mind."

"No, tell me."

"Not sure you'll like it. But, George the pirate man was recording you too."

"Doing what?" Joe knew his blush was noticeable.

"Sure...when you were fiddling with the recorder in your pocket, he was filming you with his video thing. Through that silly eye patch."

"I don't believe you."

"It's true. He was just having fun. Occasionally he

would stop one of us in the lobby or outside and show his latest 'Joe's funny videos,' which usually showed you trying to be nonchalant while encouraging people to laugh. I think he might even have won a YouTube contest for one of them."

Joe frowned. "I had no idea."

"I think at first George felt that you were making fun of his pirate persona and that bothered him because his father had belittled him for acting like a pirate."

She saw that Joe was flustered.

"Was everybody laughing at me behind my back?" he asked.

"No, of course not. Don't worry. It was all harmless, just like your laugh stuff I guess." She hesitated. "Okay, I'll see you later then."

"Sure, I'll call you," Joe said.

He closed the door and set the Compendium on the oak table. "So, I guess the pirate got me," Joe said quietly. "They all did. I wonder, was there something more to it? Were they laughing with me or at me? Who gets the last laugh? Well, wait a minute, she's right. It's all in fun. All of it."

Joe switched the recorder on and listened to Francine's laughter. At first, it wasn't uniquely distinctive. But then it exploded into a series of overlapping laughs, each one more hilarious and louder than the last. He had never heard anything so close to perfection. *Perhaps it does reflect her personality more than the other. Who am I to argue with that?*

"That's one for the ages," he said. "How do you top that? It's the zenith of laughs." Joe began to laugh, something at which he had become quite proficient. He was so loud that Mrs. Harkenstadt pounded on the wall.

Joe stopped. "So, laughs all around. Just as it should be. What a strange turn of events."

There's a Difference

When RJ told his mother that "I'm just so freaking tired of living with it," she knew he was serious.

"You don't know how much I hate people making fun," he said a few days before his appointment. "Not so much at school because they're all used to it; mainly with anyone new."

They sat at the kitchen table reviewing the authorization forms that RJ needed to complete. Alice Janeway leaned close and hugged her son. "Kids can be assholes," she said. "I remember when I was just a little younger than you, I had a terrible case of freckles and they laughed at me....."

RJ shook his head. "Okay, Mom, thanks for trying." She always attempted to mollify his frustration. "But this is me, not you, and besides, there's a difference."

RJ had his mother's freckles and red hair. However, that wasn't the issue.

He had heard the lectures that "Most people accept you for who you are" and "It's the inner self that counts" so often that he no longer listened to well-meaning relatives and loyal friends who tried to comfort him. Those bromides were little comfort when classmates pointed and whispered. One incident stood out among all the others. He was 12 years old and seriously infatuated with a cute girl named Sally. They would hold hands and walk home from school until the day when a few of her friends laughed at him. He and Sally never held hands again.

"I just want you to be sure," his mother said quietly. "You've thought about it long enough?"

RJ nodded. He had talked it over with his few close friends and reflected on what they had told him. They said it didn't make any difference to them, that he should do what makes him happy. He learned that the process itself wasn't overly complicated, although there usually was an adjustment period. He discussed it with a couple of people who had done something similar and stressed how glad they were now. His father had said that he would support RJ's final decision.

"I'm pretty sure it's the right thing to do," he told his mother.

"Has it been that bad?" she said, turning the pages of a photo album. "Your dad and I tried to make things easier. We realized we could have made the change when you were younger. We talked to other parents and considered doing something when you were about seven. But we just thought you would grow to accept it."

RJ smiled. *Not quite that easy*, he thought. He knew they were concerned; had heard them talking late at night. *I hate making them feel bad; it isn't their fault.*

"I know you meant well, but I'm tired of it. I just don't think it's going to get any better. There will always be a group of people who like to make fun of others. As much as I'm not looking forward to the procedure itself and everyone's initial reaction afterward, I think this is the best decision."

He stood and looked at the pictures on the wall. There were photos of him as a baby and throughout his adolescent years. *I do look happy there.*

"We just don't want you to have any regrets."

"Yes, I've pretty much made up my mind. Better to do this sooner than later. You will be there for the final thing, won't you?"

Alice signed the last form. "Sure, we'll be there. Wouldn't miss it. But I know you'll do fine."

"Well, I'll see you later then."

She kissed him on the cheek. "Not to worry son. Today is just a preliminary step. They like to be sure everything has been considered. I gotta run now."

After his mother left, RJ folded the papers and put them in his notebook. He sat there for a few minutes, wanting to be absolutely sure. *Am I going to regret this?* Then he looked in the hall mirror and straightened his tie.

"What a nightmare being called Rufus Jasper Janeway all your life," he said quietly. "A few pages of paperwork is worth it. I'll soon be known as Gordon, and that's a name I can live with."

Bigfoot Killed Uncle Jake

John Jacob Smith had a difficult time convincing friends that Bigfoot killed his Uncle Jake.

The first time he shared the story of his favorite uncle's death was at a campfire party when his high school friends gathered to drink beer and share urban legend tales, such as the "one armed man who almost got the teenage lovers." When John Jacob began talking about his uncle and Bigfoot, several of them laughed and then realized he was serious. He raised his right hand and explained, "This is a different type of story."

He told them that the family wasn't sure if Jake had ever actually encountered the legendary beast, but they were convinced his obsession led to his untimely death two years earlier.

"It all began in 2012 when Uncle Jake had read the first article on Bigfoot, aka Sasquatch," he said to the dubious friends. Intrigued by the alleged sightings, Jake attended a local meeting of the Bigfoot Believers (the BFB-ers). He soon had articles taped to the walls of his den, which eventually became so cluttered that it became known as the Bigfoot Man Cave.

"He heard stories that would make your hair stand up." Jake began watching TV documentaries, attending conventions, and finally going on his first BFB encounter outing in Utah's Round Valley region. "But it was when he bought the mountain cabin that pushed him to his death," John Jacob said.

Jake acquired a run-down cabin near Scipio, a small town close to their home in Gunnison. A real estate agent told him it would be the ideal place to observe Bigfoot traveling through the area. At first, his wife promised a divorce or at "least a trial separation so that you come to your senses over this insane fixation on the big furry animal." But Doris relented after realizing that his occasional absences would be a relief—less time listening to him rant about "that big hairy thing."

Jake began spending several days a month at the cabin, recording his observations, and while it didn't result in any actual encounters, he did find signs Bigfoot must have been nearby. "He had seen the footprints and large droppings that couldn't have been from any known animal," John Jacob said. "Then he talked about hearing unusual sounds late at night around the cabin. He was sure it was Bigfoot."

One of Jake's friends had pointed out that it was probably someone staging an elaborate prank that involved dressing up in an ape costume and running through the woods. "But he was convinced otherwise, and that didn't deter him from his quest," John Jacob told his campfire mates.

Jake's last trip to the cabin was just before Thanksgiving. He usually invited a fellow BFB to accompany him, but he traveled solo on this outing. Jake promised to be back for the big family dinner.

"But he never returned," John Jacob said.

"What the hell happened?" asked one of the other storytellers.

"They alerted the sheriff, but because of the Thanksgiving holiday, he wasn't able to organize a search party until the following day. It didn't take the group long to find Jake. He was seated at the base of a huge pine tree just down the road from the cabin. His legs spread out and arms folded tightly. Although they couldn't be certain, it appeared he was smiling. There was no obvious wound or sign of a struggle."

"What else did they find?" another friend wondered.

John Jacob lowered his voice. "One of the deputies noticed that Jake clutched a gob of stringy hair. Nearby there was a series of large footprints that they weren't able to identify. The sheriff and coroner agreed that it was an accidental death, but later amended it to be 'suspicious.' They said he probably had a heart attack, possibly the result of being scared out of his wits."

Two weeks after his Jake's death, they got the news from a medical lab—the hair was part human and part unknown. Meanwhile, a DNA researcher had expressed interest in doing a more thorough analysis.

"They said it could have been dog or wolf hair. Later, my father asked to see it, but he was told that the evidence bag had disappeared and from that point on, the sheriff's office denied its existence. So, we'll never know what happened that night."

John Jacob paused, looking at the group to see their reaction. A few were smiling; others were solemn. "But then it got bizarre," he continued. "After my Aunt Doris passed away, we were cleaning out her closets and found a mask and furry wolf costume."

"You're saying she was the one who dressed up and ran through the woods?" the girl next to John Jacob asked.

"Can't be certain, but does seem like it. And that opens up a whole new mystery that we're still trying to unravel. There are two theories. First, that she was trying to keep Jake interested in his hobby and give her some time alone. The other is that she wanted to scare the hell out of him. But why? We'll never know."

His friends waited for John Jacob to laugh, as they had when completing their urban legend tales. But he merely sat down and waited for the next storyteller to begin.

The Boy Who Stared at the Sun

As Sam Thorncutt's eyesight started to deteriorate, he began searching for both solutions and causes.

Of course, his first goal was to find some remedy for the cloudy vision in his right eye. But he also wanted to know why it was occurring at the age of 41.

After conversations with various specialists, Sam finally got a partial answer during an appointment with a noted ophthalmologist, who asked "Have you been out in the sun a great deal, and most importantly, for whatever reason stared directly into it? That kind of exposure could be a cause of later eye problems. We can talk about a few possible corrective procedures."

"I haven't been out in the sun much as an adult, mainly because of my fair complexion. However, I'll check on something."

On the next visit with his mother, Sam mentioned the doctor's strange question. Daisy Thorncutt closed her eyes.

"Oh, I was worried that might not be a good idea," she said slowly. "When we thought you were cross-eyed, we took you to Dr. Elgin Greene, who was highly regarded and among other things recommended that you follow the Bates method of ocular reformulation, which involved staring into the sun."

"What? You're kidding."

Sam's agitation was evident to his mother. Daisy grasped the rosary beads in her housecoat pocket. "It was supposed to be a gradual treatment with no complications expected. We would sit in the backyard, and you would spend a few minutes looking up, and then we would cover your eyes with a wet cloth."

"Did you look at the sun too?"

"No, just you," she said.

"Unbelievable."

Sam was incredulous that his intelligent and well-meaning mother could be prompted to follow such a ridiculous therapy. That afternoon, he called to arrange a meeting with the elderly doctor who now resided in an assisted living home. Two days later, he was sitting in the visitor's room waiting for a nurse to escort Dr. Greene. Sam had told her he was a reporter who wanted to write an article about the doctor's career. The nurse pushed the wheelchair so that Dr. Greene was close to Sam. She introduced them and then left.

"Would you mind taking off your dark glasses so I can see you better?" Sam asked.

"I'd prefer not to; the glare bothers my eyes," the doctor replied. "Besides, you can see most of me."

"All right then. Well, it seems as a young boy I was one of your patients, and according to my mother, you gave directions for me to stare in the sun as a partial cure for my supposed cross-eyed syndrome. What kind of quackery is that?"

The doctor cleared his throat and leaned away from Sam.

"I thought you were doing a story."

"I am…..my story. I'm a former patient who has a serious

vision problem that may be partially because you told my mother to have me stare at the sun."

Doctor Greene grabbed the armrests. "You are an angry man, that much I can tell," he said in a raspy voice. "Let me explain. The Bates method was, while somewhat controversial, a well-known procedure at the time and I only used it rarely for those cases that I found particularly troublesome, which I assume yours was."

Sam shook his head. "But as I understand, several prominent ophthalmologists discounted it as being highly unreliable and ineffective and very likely harmful. Did you explain that to my mother?"

"Well, of course, I can't recall our specific conversations, but I'm sure I outlined all the options. Your mother was most likely at her wit's end and sought relief for you that she couldn't find elsewhere. Besides, there has never been any direct evidence that the method caused permanent damage leading to blindness or any of the other eye disorders. I gave everyone obvious directions, you know—the dos and don'ts; such as look up only briefly. Perhaps you stared too long."

"That's not good enough," Sam shouted.

The doctor jerked backward. "I can understand your frustration. I've had a few patients who experienced vision maladies as adults, but they weren't connected with the Bates method. Besides, those people seemed to understand."

"You can't imagine what I'm dealing with."

Doctor Greene slumped in his wheelchair. "I think I can."

"No, I'm 41 with a career that entails reading documents and writing reports. That will be somewhat difficult when I can't see."

The doctor nodded. Sam was irritated at his unwillingness to make eye contact. "I'd like you to see this article that completely discounts the Bates method."

"No need for that."

"Yes, there is a need." Sam held the article closer.

"There's no need because you see, I've been blind for the last ten years. Imagine that, an eye doctor who can't see."

Sam lifted the glasses that covered the doctor's eyes and waved his left hand back and forth. The doctor didn't blink.

"Sorry for your loss, but that doesn't change the basic facts," he said. "You shouldn't have recommended such techniques." Sam's anger had dissipated.

"That's one regret," the doctor said. "I have others; as I imagine you do as well."

The doctor turned his wheelchair to the right. "Can you take me back to my room now?" he asked.

"I'll get your nurse."

"I'd rather have you do it."

Sam saw that the nurse wasn't there to help, so he began pushing the doctor down the hallway. As they entered the room, Sam was surprised to see it was decorated like a doctor's office. There were eye charts and photos of young children modeling glasses.

"Why do..."

"Why do I have all of those things on the wall? Simple; it reminds me of what I was once. I don't have to see everything to know that they're there. Gives me comfort."

Sam pushed the doctor closer to the couch. "Look, I guess I do understand. It was a different time."

"Well, that's something."

Sam touched the doctor's shoulder. "Okay then, I'll see you."

The doctor laughed at Sam's choice of words. "Not if I see you first."

As he closed the door behind him, Sam could hear the doctor cry, quietly at first and then much louder. *Maybe I should go back in*, he thought.

But then he walked away.

Killer Parents

Growing up, I was sure my mother and stepfather were the greatest. As a teenager, many of my friends agreed they were almost model parents. "Your parents are killer, just amazingly fun to be around," I remember my best friend Marla saying during one of our frequent sleepovers.

But that was before I learned they were murderers. As I write this, I can hardly form the letters of that word—murder. "Killer parents" no longer seems to be a good way to describe them.

I've spent the last year trying to think of anything that might have been a warning sign, some indication that they were capable of not only killing other people but their own family members. The fact that their heinous crimes occurred more than 25 years ago doesn't alter the fact that they are both homicidal sociopaths.

My mother tipped me off. "Please come over, we need to talk," she said that hot July day about a year ago. When I arrived, she began talking frantically. She looked haggard; her usual perfectly styled auburn hair in disarray.

"You're going to be hearing about this," she said in a panicked voice. "I don't have much time to explain. It's an old story for a terrible crime that I'm responsible for. But I've been a different person. I hope one day you can forgive, or at least not hate me."

She quickly told me that before she and my stepfather had married, my birth father had been a heavy drinker and often abusive. She and one of her church members, Gerald Sharp, fell in love and wanted to get married. After an exceptionally violent argument with my father, mother felt she had no other choice…but to shoot and then bury him on their farm. She contrived a story about him running away, and for some reason, their few friends seemed to believe her. "Suppose I rationalized that it was self-defense," she explained in a very excited voice. I told her to stop talking; that I couldn't process it. I began hyperventilating as if I was gagged or had a bag over my head and was suffocating. I had one of my most severe anxiety attacks ever. I had to leave. As I opened the door and ran down the walkway, I heard her call, "Please don't give up on me." I couldn't even look back.

A day later, the police came to visit and gave me the rest of the story. It seems a couple of my father's cousins eventually became suspicious and contacted the local police department. Two cold case detectives started searching for her a couple of years ago and finally matched old Social Security information with her current location. "Did your mother and stepfather ever mention anything about their backgrounds?" one officer asked.

"How was my stepfather involved?" I stammered.

"We believe Sharp killed his wife and possibly a brother-in-law so he could run away with your mother."

"I'm shocked… devastated," I said, or something like that.

After they left, I gathered letters, photos, every family memento I had in my apartment. There had to be an indication of disharmony, behavioral quirks, or something. Some clue as to how two seemingly normal people could transform into murderers.

Mother told me that my birth father had died in an automobile accident during a business trip to Idaho when I was about one year old. As I got older, I asked her about him, but she never said much, and my memories were fuzzy. I thought back to all the family gatherings over the last 25 years, and I don't recall observing severe anger from my mother or stepfather; certainly not the kind of rage that could lead to multiple murders. All I saw in the family albums were smiling faces.

After their arrests, more details came out. There were newspaper articles and lurid TV news updates. As the story unfolded with more gruesome details about what they had done, neighbors began looking at me differently, as if I had somehow been aware of their horrendous crimes. I stopped going out often and eventually started having my groceries delivered.

I began reading more about family-related homicides. I did an online search for articles about the correlation between violent parents and their equally terrifying offspring. While there was no substantial consensus among psychiatrists and others, I was scared of passing this trait on, so against my then fiancé's wishes, I had a hysterectomy. I just couldn't bear the thought of having children who might one day display violent behavior. Of course, he didn't want to marry someone who couldn't have children. We broke up, and I haven't seen him since.

I only attended the first day of my mother's trial; it was just too much. Afterward, I remained closeted in my apartment, with an occasional visit from one of my few friends. I continued to be obsessed with our family history and the propensity for violence. It was exhausting.

My mother sent me a few letters trying to explain…but how in the hell do you justify that you killed your husband so you could marry a man who killed his wife?

She and Sharp (can't call him "stepfather" any longer) eventually pled guilty to some lesser crimes, although they both received lengthy sentences. Hers was less severe because she somehow was able to use a battered wife syndrome defense. So, it's conceivable she could be out of prison in 20 years.

I, on the other hand, will likely never leave my prison… wondering if I might suddenly become angry at some perceived slight and do something terrible. My therapist assures me that this is highly unlikely, but I'm not so confident. How can I be? Afraid to date anyone, worried what he might think.

The doctor also encouraged me to write everything down in this journal so that I could share it with others. I have had a publisher express an interest in my story. But I don't know. It is so incredibly painful and personal. Also, scary because recently I seem to have become overly impatient and irritated over minor things. Not sure what to do.

Feats to Remember

The first foot washed ashore in Piney Cove four days before Memorial Day weekend. Tommy Crenshaw took a break from picnicking with his family to explore the nearby tidal pool. He reached into a pile of driftwood splinters and saw a shoelace. When he yanked the cord, Tommy lifted a soggy tennis shoe that had a foot inside.

"Oh crap," the 10-year-old towhead yelled. He flung the shoe up over his head, and it landed on a bowl of potato salad that Mrs. Alice Fenster had arranged as part of her picnic spread.

"My god almighty, there's a foot in the salad," Mrs. Fenster yelled. It didn't take long for a large crowd to gather, including Sam Bledsoe, who immediately called his brother Ed, the recently appointed Sheriff, who arrived with his deputy. Ed was a former New York police detective who left Manhattan to avoid "premature meltdown" and also get away from his angry ex-girlfriend.

As the startled picnickers looked on, Sheriff Bledsoe quickly bagged the foot and took it to Dr. Flemson for an exam.

"I know it's a human appendage doc, but I'm more concerned if you can tell what happened to it," he said as the portly coroner carefully analyzed the purplish colored flesh.

Meanwhile, the beach crowd was in a frenzy; everyone shouting theories about the newly arrived foot on a string.

"It's a fake foot."

"Is not, probably came from a morgue."

"I'll bet there's a murder involved."

And so on.

Then a day later, while Doc Flemson was still analyzing the foot, another one appeared. A surfer was wading into the ocean when she noticed the foot resting on top of a mass of seaweed. She quickly alerted Sheriff Bledsoe.

Doc Flemson now had a pair of feet on his exam table. The Piney Cove Review's two reporters heard about the latest one and rushed to his office.

Everyone agreed that this was definitely bad timing, considering the 8th annual Healthy Feet Fun Run was scheduled for the town's annual Memorial Day Extravaganza. The coffee shop chatter was now almost entirely focused on the growing foot infestation. Some said it was the work of a serial killer; others thought it might be some type of satanic ritual or human body parts trafficking.

"Much more likely that the severed feet are from a drowning victim from a boat accident or a suicide—someone jumping from the upstate bridge or even from that recent Tsunami disaster," Dr. Flemson said to reassure the sheriff, who was being pestered for answers by reporters, worried parents, and other Piney Cove residents.

When the third and fourth feet washed ashore the day before Memorial Day, Sheriff Bledsoe and Mayor Carpenter called an emergency conference.

"The papers are having a field day with us," the Mayor complained to the city council members. "What the hell is going on? Our hotels are starting to get cancellations from tourists."

"We'll get it handled," the sheriff replied. "I'm certain it's just an unfortunate coincidence."

Meanwhile, Dr. Flemson was waiting for a report from the FBI lab in Washington, D.C. The day before the Healthy Feet Fun Run, he asked Bledsoe, "Are we waiting for the other shoe to drop?" Then, realizing his unintentional pun was in poor taste, added, "What I meant was do you think we'll be getting any more feet?"

Bledsoe shook his head. "Hopefully not. We likely have one case solved. We traced the tattoo with a phone number to a man who lived in a neighboring town. According to his family, he was fishing from a bridge, fell into the river and drowned because he couldn't swim. Apparently, a boat ran over him later and sliced his foot off. Listen, I'd like to try and put this behind us. I suggest we dispose of the feet."

On race day, two runners approached the sheriff who was arranging the safety signs and directing traffic. "I understand you have had several feet wash ashore here lately," said the taller one who wore the #421 bib.

Sheriff Bledsoe moved closer to runner #421. "Yes, why do you ask?" He had become quite defensive about the town's foot collection, dreading the daily questions and jokes.

Both runners raised their right pant leg. "As you can see, we're minus one ourselves," said runner #422. They each had an artificial right foot.

Startled, the sheriff dropped the race flag. "Well, that's an unusual sight, the same missing foot and all. If you don't mind me asking, how did that happen?"

Number 422 shifted his weight to the left side. "Unusual circumstances," he said. "I was surfing just up the coast, and a shark grabbed my foot. Tore it off and I almost died from the loss of blood. His case is even stranger."

Runner 421 smiled. "I worked on a barge just off Goat Island out there," he said pointing to the distant spot of land. "I was tethered to the side, scraping barnacles and other debris when there was a huge explosion that blew me underwater. I was tangled in cords and nets weighted down with cement blocks; without an oxygen mask. I got free except for one foot that was caught in a metal cable. It was either cut the foot off or drown, so I grabbed my knife. Fortunately, the Coast Guard had arrived by then and got me to a hospital. They said what I did was quite a feat."

Sheriff Bledsoe stared at the two runners, thinking it odd and an extreme coincidence that two footless runners appeared together for the race. "You've got some stories, that's for sure. Anything I can do for you?"

Runner 421 pointed toward his partner. "Well, we would like to take a look at the feet you have stored, just to see if they might be ours. And if so, to give them a proper burial."

"There may be a problem, but I'll check."

"How so?" said #422.

The race director's call to assemble at the starting line interrupted Bledsoe's response. "We've got to run," the tall one said. And they did.

The headline in the next day's Review exclaimed:

Two Put Their Best Feet Forward to Tie Race

The story covered the run in great detail; specifically, how runners 421 and 422 arrived at the finish line together. An article several days later was of more interest to the sheriff and city council:

Two Runners Sue City for Losing Feet
--Blame Sheriff/Coroner for Premature Cremation

An even stranger situation occurred a month later when Sheriff Bledsoe lost his left foot in a serious motorcycle accident. Also, the two runners dropped their lawsuit after the city council agreed to erect a small stone monument inscribed with "To All Foot-loose and Fancy-Free People."

This may seem difficult to believe, but that's just about how it happened.

The Rainbow Lake Fishing Contest

"What do you think will win it this year?"

"Last year, it was a total of 11 pounds. I'm thinking a little more this time."

Harlow Jimerey and Baxter Bond stood at the eastern shore of Rainbow Lake, which was unusually full because of the heavy winter rains. They wore the same camo waders and overstuffed fishing vests but were otherwise an odd match. Bond was in his early thirties, tall and thin, with a full black beard and forearms wrapped in tattoos. Jimerey was nearly 60, clean shaven, with short gray hair and at least 40 pounds heavier than his companion.

"They say more have entered this year's contest than ever before," said Jimerey, adjusting his vest.

"All the more reason for us to figure out a way to win," Bond added. "The entry fees and sponsor funds make this a very nice grand prize-winning package. Plus, there's the bragging rights."

They had entered the contest for the last 10 years but never came close to finishing in the top five. And they had used some of Bond's premier strategies: adding lead weight just prior to judging (he had just read The Jumping Frog of Calaveras County), chumming, and secretly (or so he thought) fishing with two rods, all of which were illegal and would have resulted in instant disqualification and a hefty fine.

"Any bright ideas this time?" Jimerey asked.

"I do have some of Uncle Mel's special bait."

"Oh, that should get us to the winner's circle."

"Like I've told you before, there are three ways you can win this contest," Bond said. "Use your supreme fishing skill with a little luck, cheat, and a combination of skill and imagination."

They watched as the other anglers began moving to their favorite spots. Several were in bass boats of various types, while others preferred inner tube floats. Claude Simpson settled next to an oak tree, and Jack Thompson crouched behind a huge boulder.

"The contest is about to begin," the announcer shouted.

The rules for the six-hour contest were simple. The team whose two small-mouth bass weighed the most received the grand prize. Anglers had to keep their fish in an oxygenated container so that upon weighing, they could be released. And no cheating was allowed.

Thirty-three fishermen soon scattered from one end of Rainbow Lake to the other and along the Little Rainbow River. They tested various live baits and artificial lures until their first strike and then adapted their technique accordingly.

Jimerey and Bond usually started fishing together and then eventually separated so that they could try different areas. A half-hour after his first cast, Bond walked through the brush to the Little Rainbow River. Jimerey watched as several of the contestants pulled in their first fish and carefully placed them in the containers. He finally caught a small one and quickly released it.

Two hours later, Bond returned. "How have you done?" he asked.

"Just a couple mid-sizers; not trophy winners."

"I might have the prize catch for us," Bond said. He raised the lid of his container and carefully lifted a thick bass. It was much bigger than any fish either of them had previously caught.

"Jeez Louise. Where did you get it?"

"Just up the bend a bit."

Jimerey dropped his rod to the ground. "They've got to be at least eight pounds each. How did you get them? I can't believe it."

"It was a combination of Mel's bait and a different technique that I'll tell you about later."

Jimerey looked at the end of Bond's rod. There was a bass plug; it wasn't set up for bait. "You're up to something aren't you? You didn't use Mel's bait."

Bond shook his head. "You're too mistrustful. Besides, I think it's all over now."

The bell rang, signaling an end to the contest. The other fishermen began walking toward the judging stand. Bond and Jimerey got in line for the weighing.

"I'm starting to wonder again about your catch," Jimerey whispered.

"Just be ready to collect your prize."

Each angler walked up to the judges and proudly displayed their catch. As they approached the stand, Jimerey became more nervous. "If you've done something, they'll find out."

"Be confident, trust me."

They were the last to have their fish weighed. The head judge carefully weighed and measured Bond's two bass. He asked another judge to verify the weight. "Well, according to the official scale, the total here is 19 ½ pounds, and we've got a winner."

"I cry foul," shouted one of the other anglers. "Bond has been known to try something funny in the past. Perhaps he's loaded them with weight."

The judge reexamined the fish. "No weight added here."

"Well, see if they've done something else," another fisherman said.

Jimerey was fidgeting.

"Everything checks out," the judge finally said. "Congratulations to Harlow Jimerey and Baxter Bond, winners of the 15th annual Rainbow Lake Fishing Jamboree."

As they accepted the trophy and cash award, Bond and Jimerey waited for other anglers to approach. A few congratulated them; most complained and walked away. When they were finally alone, Jimerey said, "Okay, no one can hear; I want the answer. How you did it."

Bond held up three fingers of his right hand. "Well remember the three ways to win? One of them included using your imagination, which I did starting three years ago. That was when I came across an old gentleman named Fergus Montash during one of our outings. He was feeding fish in this small grotto that he had created just up the river. I stopped to talk, and he explained that he had this pen of smallmouth. Fergus explained that he had been feeding them for quite some time, the reason they had grown so large. He was quite sick and said this was his last trip to the grotto. He wanted to release them, but when I explained my idea—that I might catch them for the contest—he thought that was a grand plan, as long as they were released. So, I gave him $200, and we left two in the pen…until today."

Jimerey shook his head. "This is unbelievable."

"So, I've been coming back to feed these babies. This was the perfect time to enter them in the contest."

"But it's still cheating. We didn't actually catch them. Why didn't you tell me?"

"I knew you'd probably object; that's why I didn't tell you earlier. But no matter, it's not really cheating. All we have to do now is split the cash two ways and return home."

"You mean three ways."

They turned to see a short, bald man walking quickly from behind a tree. He had obviously overheard everything.

"I'll take my share and not say a word to anyone."

Bond laughed. "You devious snoop. Good luck, you've got no proof. Our prize-winning fish are in the river now."

"That's true, but I think you'll agree that the tape recording I have of your conversation will at the very least besmirch your reputation with the other anglers. Not sure you'll ever be invited back to this or any other Association event."

"Oh, I'm gonna be sick," Jimerey grumbled.

Bond approached the interloper. "What's your name anyway?"

"Walter Montash."

Bond shook his head. "What was your father's name?"

"You know what it was. Fergus, same as your old fisherman buddy who clued you in on his bass-growing pen."

"How did you know about today's contest and…"

"The deception? He and I had a run-in a few years back, and he decided to cut me out of his project. So, I've been watching the doings ever since and saw that you were in on this with him. Seems only right that I share in the proceeds. Wouldn't you say?"

"We could call your bluff, and you would end up with nothing. Not sure being invited back to this contest is that big of an incentive. There are other contests. Tell you what—we'll give you a one-fifth share."

Montash rubbed his hands together. "Okay, done."

Bond sat down and began dividing the money into three piles. He handed one to Montash who grabbed it and said, "Great. I'll see you next year. I'll show you the other pen, with even larger bass."

Neighborhood Watch-ing

Their cul-de-sac had ten homes, only one of which Charles Blakely and the other long-time residents were watching closely.

They had appointed Charles as the neighborhood watch commander, charged with helping new arrivals adjust to the Pleasant Manor community and, more recently, keeping tabs on Thomas Barnett, the retired college professor who had relocated from Sacramento after his wife died.

During his first few weeks there, Barnett stayed to himself, which many considered to be the main problem. He hadn't attended the neighborhood rummage sale, contributed a recipe to the annual chili cook-off, invited anyone over for coffee or a beer, or done anything else to be part of the group. Whenever he was asked to participate in the various activities, he would simply say, "Not interested. Some other time."

Two months after Barnett arrived, Charles volunteered to make one of the rare Neighbor Intervention Visits. He found Barnett sweeping his front porch. "We're a good group of people," Charles said. "Not sure just why you don't want to join us."

Barnett scratched his head. "It's nothing personal," he replied. "I'm not a joiner. Never have been. It's not my style. No offense."

"We just think you would have known that this type of neighborhood is more social than others."

"It wasn't my motivation for moving here."

Barnett then smiled and went inside his house.

"He's a loner, and we know from experience that can be troublesome," Charles reported at their next weekly watch meeting. "Still, I know how intimidating it was for us when we moved here."

"He may have something to hide," said Jack Monroe. "I suggest we do an Internet search. Charles, you're a writer who knows how to research, so this should be in your wheelhouse."

They all agreed, and Charles began his online sleuthing that evening. He sent an e-alert to everyone, explaining that his research revealed Barnett was 72, had been a tenured professor at Sacramento State University, his wife had died in an automobile accident, and he had two adult children. It appeared he had no criminal record and no civil or other judgments had been filed against him. He was leasing the house for six months.

The only time Barnett was seen the rest of the summer was when he walked his dog or worked in the flower garden. The real trouble started when he began planting large hedges in the side yard next to Mrs. Pimlet's house. She called Charles to report the offense and requested that they get together to discuss "the ramifications." Most agreed that Barnett had isolated himself as a lone wolf who would likely never fit in. But other than the hedge planting and general distrust, they were unable to pinpoint any major transgressions.

"I do think he needs to be watched more now," Harry

Ledbetter said at their mid-summer block party. They decided to add hidden cameras to the outside of their houses to be certain Barnett's actions were accurately recorded.

Three days after installing the cameras, they began calling each other to report Barnett's late-night behavior. One neighbor said he saw Barnett wandering the street, another had observed him carrying a large bag, and someone reported seeing him mow his lawn.

Charles soon learned Barnett realized they were watching him. While reviewing one evening's video replays, he noticed that Barnett would slowly approach each neighbor's camera, wave, and smile.

They discussed other options for monitoring his behavior. "Perhaps a more thorough background check, which as you recall I suggested in the beginning," said Ledbetter at the quarterly golf outing. "Who knows, perhaps he's running away from something else."

"I've got a cop friend I could check with," added Armstrong Barnes.

"Let's hold off on that for now," Charles said. "I'm concluding that he's just not an outgoing person and probably still grieving over his wife. Plus, I remember it took us a while to adjust to the social calendar."

It was during the Labor Day barbeque that they confirmed the recent change in Barnett's behavior. The neighbors hadn't seen him for several days—not walking his dog, tending the garden, or wandering late at night.

"What if he dropped dead in the house?" Mrs. Pimlet asked. "Should we have the cops do a welfare check?"

Just as Mrs. Pimlet was about to repeat her suggestion, they saw several people approach Barnett's house. A woman wearing a blue blazer with a Tip Top Realty emblem planted a "for sale" sign on the front lawn and led a man and a woman to the front door.

Charles walked over and introduced himself. "Is Mr. Barnett moving?" he asked.

"He left two weeks ago, and before leaving, he asked me to give one of you this envelope. I'm the realtor trying to sell the house. This is Mr. and Mrs. Eugene Smith who might be interested in moving here."

Charles shook hands with Mr. Smith. "You'll love it here," he said. "A very friendly neighborhood. Everyone gets along so well."

The couple smiled and followed the realtor into Thomas Barnett's former house. As he walked back to the barbeque, Charles opened the envelope and read the brief letter.

"You'll never believe this," he told the neighbors who had waited for his report. "Listen to this note from Barnett. 'Dear friends of Pleasant Manor, I'm sorry I wasn't friendlier or more engaged during my time there. I was just so busy writing. During my sabbatical from the university, I've been researching for a book on the unusual dynamics of life in a cul-de-sac neighborhood. You were all a big help in my understanding this unique culture. I witnessed some very interesting behavior over the last six months and appreciate you all being so open. Of course, I'll change the names in the book and will send you a couple copies when it's published."

"Well, I didn't see that coming," said Ledbetter.

"Hope he doesn't treat us too harshly," Monroe said.

"He said he won't use our names, so no one will know," added Barnes.

"But we will," Monroe responded.

Mrs. Pimlet clapped her hands. "Well anyway...it's time to begin planning a new welcome party," she announced. "I'm sure these new people will be wonderful neighbors."

A Wanted Man

Joe Peters drove to the side of the road along the edge of the Mississippi River in Boonville, Missouri, and shut off the engine. He looked over at his wife, who was applying her favorite red lipstick. Joe squashed his cigar stub in the ashtray.

The young couple had been traveling for several hours on their way to Chicago and were now uncharacteristically irritated with each other.

"Why here of all places?" she asked. "Are you lost again?"

Joe realized Sarah wasn't prepared for a cross-country trip. Her usual mildly pleasing disposition had gradually deteriorated into a series of cranky diatribes about the weather, his driving, and their future plans.

"I thought it would be a good place for a quick rest and I can take a few photos. That's quite a view of the Mississippi River that you don't often see."

"Oh great, more damn pictures. Just what we need."

"Give me a break, Sarah. I know you're hot and pissed off at the world and me. Let's try to make the best of the trip. We'll be in Chicago tomorrow."

"How exciting. I can't wait."

Joe got out of the car and walked down the short hill, closer to the river. There were a few clapboard cottages arranged around a grove of mangrove trees. The lone canoe created a series of gentle ripples on the river's surface. Joe had taken a few photos when he heard the loud voice.

"Don't you be taking my picture."

He turned quickly to his right and saw the burly man slowly approaching from the clearing about 100 yards away. Joe lowered the camera and waved at the man, who had a shaved head and a weightlifter's muscled arms.

"No, I'm not taking your photo. I'm doing pictures of the river, which we've never seen before. You weren't in the picture. I promise."

"I. Don't. Believe. You," he said, slowly accenting each word. "I said do not take my photo."

The man continued walking. Sarah was now standing behind Joe.

"What's going on?" she said.

"Just a misunderstanding. The man thought I was taking his photo, which, of course, I'm not."

The camera-shy man stopped about 10 yards from Joe.

"Look, he's a very amateur photographer who wasn't paying attention," Sarah said. "He's not good at directions; hence, we're obviously lost."

"I don't give a damn. You don't be taking my photo because I'm a wanted man."

Joe coughed loudly. "What do you mean by 'wanted'?" he asked.

"What the hell do you think he means?" Sarah said. "There is likely a law enforcement agency of some kind that would like to find him." Then, louder so she was certain the outlaw could hear, "It sometimes takes my husband a few extra steps to get to the right conclusion."

The man started walking toward them again. "That's right, lady, more than one bunch of asshole cops would like to find me, and I don't want people taking my photos. I like my privacy here."

Joe looked up toward the road to see if anyone else had stopped, but they were alone.

"Okay, then, we'll leave," he said.

"Not so fast; I want your camera."

"Oh, come on, I didn't take your photo, and there's been no harm done here."

Joe hadn't noticed that the man had a club in his hand. "I'm done talking. As I said, I'm a wanted man for some very bad behavior, and I want the mother fucking camera."

Joe had taken a few more steps back when he saw Sarah suddenly pull the gun from her purse and point it at the wanted man.

"Enough of this crap," she shouted. "We didn't take your damn photo, we're not giving you the camera, and you're not going to use that club."

The wanted man stopped abruptly. He stared at Sarah, both surprised and angry that anyone would point a gun at him.

"Lady, I don't expect you'll use that."

"Let's see then," Sarah shouted. "It's been a long day so far, and you've just made it even more unappealing. Now back off, and we'll be out of this Boonville place."

The wanted man was no longer swinging the club. "If I ever hear that you've told cops about this, I'll…"

Sarah waved the gun in his general direction. "Give me a freaking break," she said. "You'll have no idea where we'll be. Now, see you around, and good luck with being a wanted man."

As they quickly walked back to the car, Joe grabbed

Sarah's arm. "What the hell with the gun? We've never owned one before."

Sarah smiled. "I borrowed this thing from Connie just before we left. Thought it might come in handy."

"And you forgot to tell me?"

"Obviously. But it all worked out, right? If I hadn't, your friendly photo subject might have bashed us both."

She put the gun back in her purse and opened the car door.

"I don't imagine you have a permit," Joe asked. "Any thought as to your response in case we should get stopped for some reason, and a cop asks to look through the car?"

Sarah leaned back in the car seat and closed her eyes. "You always worry about something, don't you? We'll figure it out. If you drive carefully, we won't get stopped. Besides, I suddenly feel a whole lot better. That gave me a little extra charge. The trip just became a bit more interesting. There may be other surprises ahead."

"Wonderful," he said, starting the engine. "Can't wait to see what happens next. Can you give me a clue?"

"Well, it will be fun to see how your relatives welcome us at next week's big family gathering. There could be some dramatic reactions when they meet me, the woman they believe wrecked your first marriage."

"Promise me you won't stir up any trouble."

"You're worried about me telling them that you were the real sinner? I won't say anything unless they get too 'holier than thou' with us. Anyway, we'll see how it all goes. Now, drive."

They drove down the dirt road along the Mississippi River away from Boonville, Missouri. Sarah held her right hand out the window. When the angry wanted man saw her extend the middle finger toward him, he began running after them and then tripped over a log.

"Serves the asshole right," she said. "Kansas City here we come."

"Looks like we're back on the roller coaster again," Joe answered and lit another cigar.

Where There's Smoke

Every Saturday morning, Todd Michaels and Shawn Stevens met at the top of the grassy hill overlooking their neighborhood in Crestview. They sat on the old broken logs and planned new adventures.

The two 12-year-old pals often played marbles or traded cards. On other days, they just talked. Todd would complain that his father was too stern, and Shawn always griped about homework or his small allowance.

"What's up today?" Todd asked on the second Saturday of May. Both boys wore their L.A. Dodgers baseball caps backward.

Shawn looked down at the early morning scene below: two neighbors mowing lawns, a young boy shooting baskets, and two girls jumping rope.

"Well, I've meant to show you this lighter that I found in my brother's drawer," he said. "It has a picture of a naked lady on the side and a bright flame."

Shawn always had the coolest items, like the shrunken head his uncle had given him and the bag of old coins his brother had found in their attic.

"Let me see."

Todd examined the lighter. He turned it over, and the lady's clothes slowly disappeared. "Where do you suppose he got it?"

"Who knows where he gets some of that girly stuff."

Todd rubbed the flint switch, and a bright blue flame opened. "Wow, that is big," he said.

He was marveling at the flame's brightness when a noisy crow screech startled him. He dropped the lighter, which fell into the dry brush.

They were both surprised to see the small fire.

"You jerk," Shawn shouted. "Hurry, let's put it out."

They kicked dirt at the flames. Todd used a stick to break it up, but that only made the fire spread faster.

"Oh my God, what are we going to do?" he asked.

The morning breeze had fanned the flames, and within minutes, the fire had covered most of the upper portion of the hillside. They could see several people in the street below. One was spraying a garden hose at the front of his house; others were pointing at the fire and shouting.

"We're going to be in the biggest trouble," Shawn yelled. "We better get help."

The crackling flames were now spreading further down into the brushy canyon. There was nothing that Todd and Shawn could do, so they left. At the top of the street, they shouted to Mrs. Porter, who was approaching her mailbox. "Call the fire department," Todd cried. "We just saw a fire in the canyon."

As they ran the three blocks to their houses, the boys could hear the loud sirens. Just before they separated, Shawn said: "Don't say a word." Todd nodded and rushed a half block to his house.

"Why are you out of breath?" his mother asked.

"Fire, fire... we didn't know," he stammered.

His mother knew something was wrong and led him to

the couch. Todd told her what had happened. "Didn't mean to, didn't mean to," he kept repeating.

"Well, I'm not sure what to do," she said. "When your father gets home from golf, I'm sure he'll have a few ideas. Right now, I'd suggest you wait in your room and think about what you'll say."

She saw Todd's worried expression. "Don't fret. I think he'll be reasonable. Now, just wait until lunch."

However, Todd knew she also doubted his father's calmness. Two hours later, they sat down to lunch, and his mother said quietly, "Todd has something to say," while his brother and sister waited.

Todd started to speak, but his father stopped him. "Wait, Todd. First, I understand congratulations are in order. Ben Wagner heard from Adele Porter and told me that you reported the fire, and that kept it from being an even greater disaster. Mighty quick thinking. Now, let me tell you my story. We were driving to the golf course clubhouse earlier and saw the flames of the big fire. The other guys started talking about it, wondering how it started and such. Oliver said something like, probably a car backfire or two kids playing with matches. Then everyone began talking about kids messing around, playing with matches, and that kind of thing. I said that if one of my boys ever started something like that, I'd go ballistic. I'd give him a major good slap, make him apologize to every one of the homeowners down there, take him to the police station myself, and probably put him in military school. That's just for starters. All agreed that would be the reasonable punishment for imbeciles playing with fire. Anyway, not my boys." Mr. Michaels winked at the two brothers.

Todd shifted in the chair. His face was flushed, and he felt queasy.

His father leaned forward and smiled. "So Todd, what did you want to tell us?"

Todd looked at his mother for reassurance and, seeing none, turned to his father. Then he gagged, vomited on the serving plate, fainted, hit his head on the floor, and never woke up again.

Shawn later called to express his sympathy for Todd's death. The following May, the Stevens family moved away from Crestview.

After high school graduation, Shawn became a member of his local volunteer fire department.

The Dead Letter

The thick envelope Corley Johnston received on Valentine's Day of 2014 was from a cousin she hadn't talked to in at least six years.

"Wow this is unbelievable," she said, reclining on her living room couch.

It was a round-robin letter from eight different authors so far, each one writing something before sending it on for the next person's message. She turned the pages and saw that there were notes from seven cousins and one aunt. Most of them had not spoken to each other for several years because of slights real and imagined and most notably because of some major family upheaval that her mother always said was "way too complicated to unravel now." The first three letters were brief summaries of marriages, graduations, divorces, and other family news. The fourth one highlighted the family conflict and set the tone for the remaining correspondence.

"This should keep me entertained for a while."

. . . .

Dear "Family,"

I think this round-robin letter is rather unusual (you have heard of the Internet and e-mail, haven't you?), but I won't be the one who doesn't follow through. There probably will be others who will do that. I'll be interested to see who—if anyone else—also writes.

I can remember our last gathering when some of us tried to learn about the reasons our extended family became so fractured. We were at that reunion picnic in Denver about six years ago. There was some hushed talk between the older relatives, mainly aunts, and uncles. It seemed like they were rehashing something that had occurred a few years earlier. The cousins couldn't hear what was going on.

I was too young to get much of it, but I do know that something bad had happened.

Cousin Sam

....

Dear everyone,

Hope you're all well—at least most of you.

Quite a surprise getting this. I didn't think we'd ever connect again. Interesting to see how all it takes is one major family incident to keep most of us estranged.

Not sure if we can ever arrive at any resolution. As I understand, it was Grandfather Jon who ordered the few who know what happened to keep it quiet.

Anyway, Cousin Bill and I believe that someone in the family has done something illegal, involving a car accident—which I think occurred in the summer of 2003—and got away with it. I believe that the aunts and uncles disagreed on what should be done—to turn him or herself in or to let it go. Grandfather Jon ordered everyone to be quiet, and after he died, no one was willing to do anything except go on with their own lives. And most of us haven't talked since then.

While I don't expect any family reunions in the near future, you're welcome to visit me in Chicago.

Love Alice

. . . .

Dear Cousins and others,

You'll see that I'm not signing this and... I'm a member of the family but don't want to be harassed after I tell you what I know. Interesting that Alice called it a "car accident." What she didn't mention was that the hit and run also involved a serious injury, leaving a boy brain damaged and his family in financial hardship and emotional devastation. I know because I've talked to the one who was responsible. This person (I didn't say whether it was he or she) explained that they tried to turn themselves in, but their parents were so concerned about the ramifications—not getting into college, etc. And they asked the grand godfather what to do. He said to let it pass, that there was nothing to be done about it. Let it go, my ass.

A concerned Cousin

. . . ..

Dear Family,

I'm hopeful that this letter—as old-fashioned as it might be—might contribute just a little bit to the healing.

As one of the aunts involved in the discussion, I wish we had done more to resolve it then. What an awful night that was. First, learning about the accident in which one of the cousins was involved and then the heated arguments that ensued as we tried to figure what to do. It wasn't only my father (grandfather Jon)—who, by the way, wasn't nearly as dictatorial or mean-spirited as some of you have described him—but also a few of the other adults. They shared some of the responsibility as well—because the 4th of July party had lots of open liquor bottles that some of the younger cousins sampled. One of them got drunk, decided to drive to a store for some reason, and caused the accident. So, there was lots of guilt involved.

I was told that there was no specific evidence, so the police were unable to find out who hit the boy.

Since I also have not been in contact with most of you, I too am not convinced that we can ever put this completely behind us. I can only hope that we can somehow get the situation handled correctly and once again be a family. Even though we don't see each other often, it's still important to be connected.

Aunt Connie

. . . .

Dear All of You,

It was me. I was the 14-year old who drank too much, got in my dad's car, drove to the store and on the way back had the terrible accident and ran into that boy who was riding his bicycle. I did stop, saw that he was alive, and then I called for an ambulance at the gas station.

When I got home, I explained what happened, and my parents told a couple of others, and then there was a huge argument, and I remember us leaving the party. Then I was sent to that boarding school in Connecticut for high school. My parents never discussed it with me in any detail, but they divorced a year later. I haven't talked to my father for quite a while.

I think it was one of those things that just snowballed. The parents kept quiet; grandfather Jon thought he was right in hiding it, and then those who knew realized they were involved in a cover-up too. They became too embarrassed and scared to talk with each other. I thought that the police would figure out who was driving and come after me, but that never happened.

I later learned that the boy was disabled. I've felt so terrible ever since. My guilt became enormous. I have had a huge drug problem and have been in counseling for several years. Of course, that doesn't change the horrible facts or infer that I deserve any sympathy. It just explains things a little.

I'm writing this as I prepare to meet with the local police. My attorney says that because I was a juvenile at the time, my sentence could be a little lighter. Obviously, it won't be as severe as what that boy has gone through.

I hope you can all forgive me and each other. Also, pray that the one of you who begged me to drive and was with me during the accident and ran away that terrible night (and never said a word about their involvement) has handled things better than I have. Have you felt guilty too?

Stephen P

. . . .

Corley placed the last letter on the coffee table and lit a cigarette.

Suppose I should add my letter too, she thought. *Not sure which way to go. If I write that I have felt guilty for being in the car with Stephen, even though he doesn't have the facts right, then mother will be super upset, to say the least. What purpose does that serve?*

She began writing her own letter.

Dear Johnson Clan,

This will be a short note as I'm late for a doctor's appointment and want to get this in the afternoon mail.

As Aunt Connie suggested, we need to stay connected and be a family (no matter how far apart) again. We should support Stephen in any way possible and begin to put the terrible event behind us. Besides, I think we all share some of the guilt, for not discussing this earlier and trying to resolve the situation.

I look forward to seeing many of you on my cross-country trip this summer. Meanwhile, my love to all.

Corley

Buried With His Motorcycle

Nobody knew what Gerald Shaw was building in his outdoor workshop. The first to notice was young Lawrence Poindexter who watched a truck deliver wood, plexiglass, metal sheeting, and other supplies.

Shaw had covered the shed windows with newspaper, so Lawrence was unable to sneak a peek, as he did when trying to uncover other neighborhood mysteries. But he did make several return visits, finally finding a small uncovered portion of the window pane.

"I think he wants me to see what he's doing," Lawrence told his older brother. "So far, all I see is him hammering and sawing on a big frame thing."

The suspense was over when Shaw stopped work one day and explained. Lawrence saw him in front of the shed and asked, "What are you building?"

"Everybody a little curious, are they?" Shaw said, adjusting thick bifocals. He brushed the curly white hair from his forehead and added, "Son, you'll be the first to know. I'm making a special display case." And he limped away.

Lawrence wasted no time in telling his friends about Shaw's project. "Said he's building some big box, which is pretty weird," the boy announced.

Two days later, the small window opening was

completely blocked, preventing Lawrence from any further viewing. That didn't stop him from making his regular reports. "I understand Mr. S has been collecting moon rocks and other strange things and is going to show them off in his big box, or something like that," he told his friends.

As Lawrence's sketchy updates became less frequent, the neighbors gradually lost interest. However, everyone was intrigued when Shaw unveiled his display case about six months later. It was the annual Fourth of July parade that marched down Center Street, where nearly everyone had gathered to watch the two bands, several homemade floats, groups of young bicyclists, jugglers, flag twirlers, and other enthusiastic participants.

The first spectators to see it were those sitting in their lawn chairs in front of the Piggly Wiggly Store. Three motorcycles suddenly appeared from a side street, followed by a truck that carried Shaw's burial casket. It was a huge wooden structure with two large windows, which enabled the crowd to get a good look at him. Shaw sat on his cherry red Harley Davidson motorcycle, gloved hands holding tightly to the handlebar grips. A bright blue bandana covered his head, and he wore his World War II aviator glasses.

The judges were as surprised as everyone else; Shaw wasn't included in the parade program. Many people were even unaware that he had died.

"Oh my God, is that Mr. Shaw?" an older woman asked.

"Is he waving?" another wondered.

"Is he dead?"

"I don't see him moving, that's for sure."

"Why would he do this?"

"It seems in rather poor taste if you ask me."

The spectators forgot about their child's appearance in the high school band or their neighbor riding the unicycle. They concentrated on Gerald Shaw, recently deceased motorcyclist.

As Shaw and his entourage approached the main viewing stand, the judges began discussing how to handle this unexpected development. "I'm thinking we should stop the parade and remove it," one complained.

"That will just cause more commotion," another judge responded.

Their debate was interrupted when the truck hit a large pothole. The axle broke, causing the trailer to lurch forward, and the oversized casket slid off. It landed about 10 feet from the judges, who now had a bigger decision to make.

"There will be a temporary halt while we confer about this unfortunate situation," the head judge shouted over the loudspeaker.

A boisterous crowd had gathered around the stalled casket. They saw that Shaw was smiling and had a sign around his neck that proclaimed, "I love a parade." A policeman tried to move them away, but people were insistent on getting a closer look.

Shaw's son and daughter finally arrived to take charge. Tom wanted to fix the truck so that his father could continue riding in the parade, but the driver said it would take too much time. Claire was adamant that his trip was over. "This is so embarrassing," she said. "It's one thing to have a fantasy, and I suppose that it would have been fine if he had made it through the entire parade. But do you think he would enjoy being pointed and laughed at?"

They agreed to have the casket trucked four blocks away to the Middletown Cemetery, where Shaw had already arranged for a triple size burial plot, right next to his late wife, Mildred. Tom and Claire gathered their families and a few of their friends attending the parade for the impromptu ceremony.

Tom's eulogy was simple: "He was a great, sometimes eccentric father who did it his way. We'll miss him and his offbeat sense of humor." Claire was sobbing loudly.

Tom pointed to the gravestone. "Who did that? I never knew that was prepared." Claire didn't answer.

The gravestone read: *Loving father, son, and parade sweepstakes winner. He rode and played hard.* And then in smaller type: *And fooled two of the people most of the time.*

"I wonder what he meant by that," Tom said. "Who did he fool?"

"It's pretty obvious isn't it?" Claire answered. "Until recently, did you know he was building that big burial box? I sure as hell didn't. And living in a different state, we didn't even know he was that sick. That was another secret."

Tom watched as the workmen lowered his father's casket. "You're right," he said. "Dad never let me in the shed and I stopped trying. When I asked, he said he was making a coffee table for us. When I spoke to the funeral home director earlier this week, he said that all the arrangements had been made and they would have the service tomorrow and then burial afterwards here. I certainly didn't know he had planned to be in the parade."

"Well, looks like we are a pair of fools," she said.

"On the other hand, it could have meant that he was fooling his latest two girlfriends, neither of whom knew about the other."

Claire smiled. "It was just like him to leave us hanging like this."

Three Guys Enter a Bar; Two Get Lost

Their hopes of having a friendly, relaxing getaway to San Felipe faded after about an hour in the Los Hermanos Cantina. Stan, John, and Norton sat around the small round table in the crowded and noisy bar. Stan and John had been drinking Dos Equis beer for the last hour, while Norton sipped a glass of water.

"Come on Norton, relax; it's Easter break," Stan said loudly. "We're going to get you drunk, so enjoy yourself."

John nodded. "That's right, Norton. This will be one to remember."

"You guys are becoming a pain in the ass." Norton was irritated, but not sure just why. He had thought the weekend trip would help bring the once close friends back together. They had convinced him that this would be an "epic" excursion.

John and Stan continued to drink, laugh, and try to get Norton inebriated. At one point, they were interrupted when a florid-faced man approached them. He held a battery with wires attached to two metal posts. "You need this maybe?" he smiled.

"What the hell is that?" John asked.

"I think it's an electrical charge that is supposed to give you an erection if you're too drunk to get one before visiting the whorehouse next door," Stan said.

Later, Stan and John were so engrossed in talking with two girls at a nearby table that they didn't notice Norton was no longer there.

After another two beers, Stan asked, "Hey, is Norty still in the bathroom? He's been there a long time."

"He's probably outside waiting for us to go back to camp," John said. "We should probably go."

They walked unsteadily through the swinging doors into the fading sunlight. The two local policia standing across the street laughed as the drunken friends stumbled down the steps. Norton wasn't waiting for them.

"Looks like he left us," Stan said. "Let's start walking back home."

"You remember how to get back? I wasn't paying attention."

"I wasn't either, but it shouldn't be that difficult to follow a road."

During their first 20 minutes walking along the dirt road, John and Stan were laughing about the day's activity.

"I don't think Norty is having as much fun as we are," John said.

"He'll come around. He has to loosen up a bit and forget about Jocelyn."

"Right; he's taking himself way too seriously."

"Don't think we overdid it?"

"No way."

Near the one-mile marker, it suddenly seemed darker and colder, as rain clouds covered the sky. They both had cuts on their bare feet.

"That's probably our place over there," Stan said, pointing to a distant campfire.

"Sure it is."

They finally reached the campground gate and walked quickly to what they thought was their tent. Stan sat in an empty chair and grabbed a beer from the nearby cooler. But their sudden presence startled the actual residents.

"Hey boys, what are you doing?" shouted the man as he grabbed a long pipe.

"Whoopsie, this isn't our house at all," John answered. "Don't see Norty or the van."

"Yes, we're sorry for the intrusion," Stan said to the wary camper.

They quickly retreated to the main road.

"I think we took the wrong fork back there," Stan said.

"Let's go back and retrace our steps."

An hour later, Stan and John were still retracing. They walked along the edge of a narrower path overlooking the valley where the three different campgrounds were located. They jumped back when a car full of boys drove close and stopped just long enough to throw garbage at them.

It was much colder now. Stan had fallen into a cactus bush and had several spines stuck in his right arm.

"This isn't fun anymore," John said quietly.

"I haven't been in the fun mode for the last two hours. We're lost, real lost."

"You know, if you hadn't pissed Norty off, he wouldn't have left, and we wouldn't be in this spot," John said.

"So, it's my fault that he got upset? Had nothing to do with you laughing at his haircut or that damn sign you put on his back?"

John lit a cigarette. "Screw you; we didn't want to bring you along anyway."

"What? The trip was my idea."

"Maybe, but we were trying to think of a way to do it without you."

"Go to hell."

Just as they approached a bend in the road, an SUV moved quickly toward them. Anticipating another garbage toss, Stan grabbed a stick and John had a rock. The van continued and then stopped abruptly. They couldn't see through the tinted windows.

"Who's there?" Stan shouted.

"Back off," John cried.

"Cretins. Fuckoffs. I should have left you here for good."

"Norton, is that you?" asked Stan. "What a relief. We've been walking for a while. We were sure you've been looking for us."

"We didn't think you meant to leave us in town," John added. "It's been a tough couple of hours."

"Get in the van," Norton ordered.

They climbed in the back. Stan offered a high five salute, but Norton ignored him.

"Can't believe you left us like that," John said. "Why are you so mad?"

Norton braked, and they lurched forward. "You can't remember? You know where I was for three hours? In jail. One of you taped a sign on my back that said 'Everyone here are putas and buttwads.' The bar owner didn't like it, and neither did the head cop of this nice town. So, when I went outside to get away from you drunken jerks, I was escorted to the jail, along with the van. I was in a cell with some supremely drunk people and had to pay $40 to get released."

Stan and John were tempted to blame the other for

Norton's predicament, but realized he was in no mood for excuses. They were silent during the drive back to their camp.

On the trip home the following day, they stopped at the border crossing and a guard asked, "Do you have anything to declare?"

"Yes, I'm riding with two class A assholes," Norton answered.

The guard smiled. "Of course, I meant any merchandise to declare, but I get your reference." He looked at the front license plate and raised his right hand. "Hold on, seems we have a notice from the San Felipe police chief asking us to detain a John Jessop and Stan Riley for causing great mischief in his town. My instructions are to collect on his $100 warrant or hold you here."

"How did they know our names?" Stan asked.

"No way," John said.

Norton laughed. "Thought you'd have a little fun with me?"

"You gave him our names?" John said.

"Better ante up boys or I'll have to leave you behind," Norton replied.

"Can't believe you did that Norton," Stan complained.

They pooled their remaining cash and handed the guard $85. "If I were you two, I wouldn't return to San Felipe," he advised them.

It was the last trip they would take together.

Sticks, Stones, & Internet Lies

P aul Bailey had never thought about running away or harming himself before. It was the latest online rumor that pushed him into such a dark place.

He and his parents had done everything they could think of to stop the harassment from his classmates and people he didn't even know. Now, he sat on the ledge of Suicide Bridge, near the railroad tracks that ran just behind the town of Safe Haven. The bridge was named for the two couples who had jumped to their deaths 15 years earlier.

Paul held on to the railing and closed his eyes. *How did I get here?* he wondered. *Didn't have to happen. If only they had left it alone.*

The bullying wasn't because of his small size, thick glasses, or extreme shyness. It began two months earlier when Paul told a girl he liked her, but a previous boyfriend resented his attention. The boy and his friends started taunting him during PE class and after school. Then they added comments on Facebook, stating that "Paul Bailey doesn't like girls and is a sissy boy," and he began receiving text messages from other students. "Seems that nearly everyone was in on the joke, although most of them have no idea how it got started," he told his father.

His parents asked teachers and the principal to discipline

the students, some of whom belonged to the Best Boys group. But by then, it had all snowballed so quickly that it was too late. Even a few of his oldest friends had stopped talking to him, afraid that they too would be caught up in the mess.

He heard a noise below and saw a man dressed in overalls and a straw hat.

"What are you doing up there?" he shouted.

"Just sitting," Paul said.

"What's your name?"

"Paul Bailey."

"Bailey. You're the son of George and Thelma?"

"Yes, who are you?"

"I'm Lou, the tower and bridge groundskeeper. My main responsibility is keeping young people from writing graffiti."

"Oh."

"Say, are you the boy who has been in the paper, about other kids making fun of you?"

Paul was quiet. He had forgotten about the article on high school bullying.

"Are you that Paul Bailey then?"

"How many are there? But, yes that's me."

"What are you doing up there? Are you upset now?"

What a stupid question, Paul thought. "Yes, of course."

"Not going to jump, are you? Should I be calling someone?"

"No, not now."

Lou began waving at Paul.

"Well, why not come down then."

Paul was getting cold; he hadn't brought a jacket. *Probably should climb down now.*

"Maybe soon."

Lou set his shovel aside. "Listen, you can't let those bozo goofballs get to you. They're the losers in all of this."

"How so?"

Lou hesitated, unsure what else to say.

"Because you know you're in the right and they are the creeps, and you will be able to get over it." Lou had moved closer to the ladder. "Anyway, come on down, and I'll get you a soda."

Paul watched Lou hold a cell phone. He was tired and ready to leave the bridge. "This isn't doing me any good," he said.

"Yes, you're right on that," Lou said. "So, come on down."

Paul stood and stepped carefully over the railing. As he reached down for the long ladder, Paul slipped and fell forward. His foot caught between the two rails, and he now hung upside down 60 feet from the ground.

"Help," he yelled.

"Oh my God," Lou cried. "I'll call for help."

Paul tried to pull himself up, but he didn't have the strength. *Great, now there will be another reason for people to laugh.*

He soon heard the sirens, and then the first fire truck arrived. "Hold on, son, we'll have you down in a few minutes," a young fireman announced.

"Please hurry," Paul said.

A group of kids had followed the fire truck and gathered below the bridge.

"Hey, is that Paul Bailey up there?" he heard a boy shout.

"Yeah that's him," someone else said. "Wonder how he got like that."

Oh crap, my photos will probably be on Facebook by tomorrow.

The fireman helped Paul onto the ladder. As he slowly climbed down, Paul saw several of his classmates gathered near Lou. Paul stepped on the bottom rung, and a pudgy boy extended his hand. Paul backed away from Peter Klein, the leader of the Best Boys who had made his life miserable during the last few months.

"Hey, Paul," he said. "Listen, about all that other stuff. I didn't mean anything by it. We were being jerk faces."

"Sure, whatever," Paul said, too tired and embarrassed to argue.

Peter nodded. "Anyway, it wasn't my idea; Jack Spire started everything. He's always been such an ass. You know, I was thinking, we could get back at Spire by making up something really good about him. I've got some ideas."

That would be one way for them to know what it's like. Then next time, maybe they'd think twice before pushing people like me.

"Let me think about it," Paul said. "I'm not really in the mood to talk now anyway."

"Okay then, but let me know soon," Peter said and walked away.

Paul saw him approach the other Best Boys who were laughing and shaking hands. *Of course, I wouldn't want Jack Spire to suffer as much as I have.*

Lou walked over and put his arm around Paul. "Your

father just arrived to give you a ride home. See, I told you things could work out."

"Perhaps it will get better now," Paul said. "I have some thinking to do."

Bastard Boy Bob

"Robert, it's so good to hear from you. It's been a few weeks. We've missed you since you moved to California."

"I'm relatively fine, mother. However, I do have a question for you."

"Certainly, son. What is it?"

"Why didn't you tell me I am a bastard?"

"Robert, what a terrible thing to say. Why would you ask that?"

"Well guess what happens when you apply for a certain government job? They ask for your birth certificate. And, realizing I didn't have a copy of mine, I had to visit the Social Security office. Long story short, we eventually located records showing you listed as the mother, but there was an 'unknown' for the father. And on the children's section, it first said 'no name,' which was crossed out and had Robert penciled in. So it seemed to me that you weren't married when I was born, and I'm just guessing, but it's likely that the man I've been calling dad for the last 35 years isn't my father."

"Robert…"

"Call me Bastard Boy Bob. I like the alliteration."

"Stop it. Let me explain."

"Please do."

"Oh, I knew we should have discussed this so long ago.

Anyway, about 40 years ago, I had a boyfriend; thought we were going to be married. And it just happened."

"By 'happened' you mean you got pregnant, your boyfriend—my biological father—disappeared, you gave birth, there was some indecision about keeping and naming me, and then eventually you got married and let me think John was my real father."

"You make it sound so cold."

"The cold part was never telling me anything. You can understand why it's taken me a bit by surprise. You've got two other children with John. For some reason, he didn't think enough of me to go through the formal adoption process. I asked an attorney friend to check around; that's how I know I'm not an official Peterson."

"This is too much. I'll get your father on the phone; he can explain better."

"Robert, it's your dad. I've been listening; your mother is quite upset about this."

"Hello, John. You can call me Bastard Boy Bob."

"Cut the crap, son. You make it sound as if we planned to hurt you. That's not the case."

"Okay, we'll forget all the other stuff. Why didn't you ever adopt me?"

"Oh hell, haven't I always treated you like my son?"

"Reasonably well, although now I'll have to think back a little harder. But my question was, why didn't you adopt me?"

"It was always my intent to do so. Had the paperwork, started making plans, but honest to God, things just got in the way, and then time passed. Obviously, it was a huge mistake, but it wasn't on purpose."

"Well John, that is a rather flimsy explanation."

"So, one day you're calling me dad, and because of a piece of paper, now you're calling me John as if the last 35 years hadn't happened?"

"I think there's more to it. Did you resent Mom for having a child?"

"Of course not. But I resented your real father because he also had an affair, with my then fiancé. That was after he had been with your mother."

"Hold on."

"Yes, it is more complicated than you might imagine. After he left for good, your mother and I got together, probably consoling each other at first. Then we fell in love."

"I was only one or two, so probably a nuisance for you. You hated my father and maybe saw him in me. You tried your best to treat me like a real son, but it was probably harder than you imagined."

"There was probably some of that. But it wasn't my intent. In fact, your father blocked my initial adoption petition somehow. He wasn't being a father but didn't want me to try. It took your mom a very long time to get over everything; she nearly had a breakdown. I vowed that we wouldn't discuss the matter again, however ill-advised that might have been. We didn't look into the future to imagine how it might come back at us."

"This is hard to process. I wasn't aware of this at all. A definite change in the family dynamics. And where is my real father?"

"He died five years ago in a bar fight. That's all we know."

"Wow, another big surprise. Now I'm stumped…where the hell to go from here. There are still some missing pieces."

"First, you still have a mother and a very committed stepfather. Seems we have some talking and forgiving to do."

"I'll say. We need to sort this out. To get started, I'd like you to begin the adoption process next week."

"Really… you want me to adopt you now?"

"I think that would be nice."

"Okay, I can start working on that. What else?"

"Tell Mom that Bastard Boy Bob is gone. Also, that my attorney discovered she might have another illegitimate son."

"What?"

"Guess you didn't know that. We can discuss it later."

"Hold on, Robert."

"Bye, Dad. Talk to you next week."

The Club Lied

As he looked through the peephole, Shawn Roberson knew he might regret opening the front door of his apartment. Ralph Montgomery and Gordon Smythe stood on the other side, and Shawn wasn't sure he was in the mood for their antics.

"Oh, what the hell," he said and opened the door.

"Hi, guys, what are you up to today?"

"We're here to invite you to join our new club, but you've got to go through the initiation, just like we did," Ralph said.

"Interesting…and who initiated you?" Shawn asked.

Ralph laughed. "No matter; now are you with us?"

Shawn knew the pair often created elaborate escapades that involved their other friends. Some of these events were more unusual than others. But he didn't have classes that day and thought it could be an interesting experience.

"All right, let's go."

"Good choice," Gordon said.

They blindfolded Shawn and led him to the car. Ralph pushed him into the back seat, and they drove away.

"Hey, where are we going?" Shawn asked.

"It's a secret; you'll soon see."

As he sat in the back seat, Shawn listened to Gordon's whispered directions to see if he could tell where they were. *It doesn't seem like we're on the freeway*, he thought.

A half-hour later, the car suddenly stopped, the doors

opened, and they led Shawn out. He could hear grinding machinery and loud bird screeches. Shawn reached for his blindfold, but Gordon held his hand. "Be patient," he said.

Shawn felt something draped over his shoulders and a hat placed on his head.

"Stand at attention, new initiate," Ralph said.

As Shawn patiently waited for the next command, he heard a car engine start. He lifted the blindfold off and was startled to see they were standing in a very smelly section of the county's largest dump site. There were huge mounds of trash that attracted flocks of hungry seagulls. Even more alarming was that the three of them were dressed as seagulls, wrapped in bed sheets and wearing caps attached to large feathered covered wings. He saw Ralph in the driver's seat of the car.

"Wow, this is the craziest thing I've ever seen or been involved in," Shawn said, adjusting his feather hat. "You guys have outdone yourselves this time. But hey, where are you going?"

As Gordon walked towards the car, he slipped on a mound of seagull droppings and fell backward into a small crater.

"Help me out of this muck," he cried.

"Holy shit, how did you get down there?" Ralph asked.

"I slipped, you asshole. Now help me out."

The bulldozer driver didn't see Gordon lying in the muck and proceeded to drop a massive scoop of rotting garbage, newspapers, cans, and other refuse on him. Gordon tried to climb out of the pit, but he dislodged a cement block, which then landed on his right foot.

"Oh my God, it feels broken."

The truck driver stopped to help. "I didn't see him there," he shouted. All three of them reached down to pull Gordon from the soggy mess.

The driver looked at the three seagull men and laughed. "Not sure what your game is boys, but you seem a little out of place. Also, from the look of his foot, you should head to the hospital now."

Gordon brushed the garbage from his bird costume. Ralph helped him into the car and Shawn climbed in back. They started to leave the dump.

"Where were you going when I was standing back there like a freaking giant bird?" Shawn asked. "Seemed like you were getting ready to drive off."

"There is one thing we forgot to tell you," Ralph said.

"Not now," Gordon said.

"He should know. Shawn, there is no seagull club. The idea was to have you blindfolded so we could leave you there. We'd go and let you get back on your own."

Shawn pulled his seagull cape off.

"Why the hell would you do that?"

They were driving faster now.

"To get back at you," Ralph said, while Gordon moaned.

"For what? What have I done to you guys?"

"Oh, screw it. You didn't let us see your mid-semester exam in Engineering 102. As a result, we both got D's, which won't help our GPAs."

Shawn laughed. "You two are amazing. I didn't know you were trying to see. Besides, I would have told you not to follow my example. I didn't study and got a C- myself."

Ralph whistled. "Well, that does seem to change things. I knew we should have mentioned the test first."

"Getting a D on the test could be the least of your worries. You guys probably didn't know that Professor Anderson has a camera in his room so that he can record everything that goes on—including your previous cribbing from each other's tests and the numerous times you've flipped him off behind his back. I'll bet he factors that behavior into your final grades."

"You're kidding," said Ralph. "Why didn't you tell us?"

"You mean like you told me about the purpose of today's adventure?"

"We'll sort this out later," said Ralph. "Let's finish the initiation before we get to the hospital. So, welcome to the high order of the Immaculate Seagull Club of Bird Brothers. This is a special bond unlike any other. As a fledging member of our society, you are committing yourself to loyally following the precepts, edicts, and various other rules and regulations, most of which we haven't written. You are sworn to secrecy and will not squawk a sound of this to friend or enemy. Do you hereby agree?"

"I do. And I also promise to only let a few of our closest friends see my cell phone video of you two crazy birds acting like major assholes at the dump."

The Missing Guest

A large group of college friends, relatives, former work associates, and yacht club members had gathered at the Good Friends Pub for Jim Raymond's surprise birthday party. They were lined up along the bar, ready to shout their greetings to the guest of honor.

"I talked to him last week," said Bob, a former roommate.

"Maybe he misunderstood the directions," added Jane, Jim's favorite masseuse.

"So typical; he's always late or a no-show," said Linda, a marina waitress.

They played cards, reminisced, and drank a lot for two hours, waiting for him to enter the bar, yell his famous "Jim is in the house and now the party begins," and hug everyone.

Just as many guests were becoming increasingly impatient for Jim's arrival, co-host John whispered to Janice, who started to cry.

"Well, something's wrong," said Bob, noticing her outburst.

"Wonder if he's not coming, or maybe he was in an accident," Charlie said.

John held up his hands to stop the music and conversations. "Everyone, I've got terrible news. We just found out Jim is dead. Oh my God...he killed himself."

There was an immediate outbreak of gasps, moans, and expletives.

"What the hell," cried Bob. "What happened? Why?"

Everyone gathered near Janice and John. "Seems he took a lot of pills last night," John said. "His neighbor found him."

John's surprise announcement prompted a stream of new comments.

"Unbelievable."

"Someone here must have known."

"What a selfish act."

"That's too simplistic...you never know."

"He had everything...a bunch of friends, enough money, a nice condo."

"Jim had friends but was still lonely. Nobody to come home to at night."

"Was he sick?"

"He never got over the loss of his sister and father."

"But he was okay when I saw him last."

"Peter knew him best."

"So, it's my responsibility to know he might do this?"

"Hold on," John interrupted. "A box was just delivered."

He handed it to Janice. She opened the box and removed a letter. "Dear friends and remaining relatives," she read. "On the chance you are having that surprise party for me, I thought we could shift it to a memorial celebration instead. Sorry to have changed the focus. I know it's upsetting and perhaps surprising. But see, I'm so damn tired and want to see my family again. Anyway, the enclosed items should prompt some interesting conversation. I love you all. And remember, I tried."

Janice spread the items out on the bar counter. There was a football game ticket, a fishing lure, a Christmas tree ornament, a high school class ring, and a large bronze key.

Each one was numbered and had a label with one of their names.

"I guess those of us named have a story to tell about these objects," said John, Jim's fraternity brother. "So, I'll start. Here's a football game ticket with my name on it. I'm trying to remember the significance. Oh, yeah, it was our junior year, and State was in the championship game at the Rose Bowl. We carpooled there. I remember Jim had such a great time. Dancing on the table at the post-game party. He was the original life of the party when he wanted to be, which must have been his disguise. Funny thing, as long as I knew him, he never shared that much about his life, what he actually felt. We thought we knew him, but really didn't, and I kind of think he liked that."

Some smiled, but most were still in shock.

"The second thing is his high school class ring. Here, Peter."

The former track star looked closely at the tarnished ring. "Wow, this is hard. Guess I knew him the longest, back to our freshman year in high school. We were on and off again friends throughout the last 25 years but tried to stay in touch. He always seemed so worried about his future, whether or not he would get a good job or be able to keep it for long. One of Jim's favorite phrases was 'I'm not making my age yet,' referring to his focus on being adequately compensated. I feel bad that I haven't seen or talked to him for the last few years. I had no idea he would have done this, or I would have said something." Peter began to cry.

John handed the fishing lure to Bob. "We were fishing buddies," he said. "Went a couple of times a year. We didn't catch much but talked a lot. The thing I remember most was his telling me over and over how much he wanted a wife and kids, and yet seemed incapable of having a long-term relationship. I asked him why that was but could never get a straight answer. Sometimes he'd say that his previous girlfriends didn't understand him, and that would doom a marriage, but other times he'd explain that he was probably best on his own. I recall once suggesting that a counselor might be able to offer some good advice. Jim didn't like that idea. I think he gave up on finding someone when he turned 45."

"Next is Jane who has this ornament." She had arrived from work and still wore her Your Favorite Masseuse t-shirt. Jane cradled the small Christmas ornament in her hands. "Jim would come and see me once a month, mainly just to talk…with an occasional massage. He seemed very lonely at the holidays. Last year, I bought this Star Trek ornament, because Star Trek was his favorite TV show. I stopped by Jim's condo after work one December evening, so he could add it to his Christmas tree. But there was no tree or any other decorations, or hardly anything else, except for a few pieces of furniture. Other than a photo of his parents and sister, there were very few personal mementos, and he had lived there for several years already. There was one thing that caught my attention—a framed collage with photos of many of you that had a post-it note that read, 'Friends are and know the best.' He hung the ornament on the frame. Jim thanked me and said, 'I just wish…' and stopped. When I asked him what the wish was, he just said, 'Doesn't matter.' I should have stayed longer and talked to him more."

The last item was an oversized gold colored key. "This one is mine," Janice said. "I remember when he bought it at a garage sale not that long ago. I asked why it was important, what the key meant to him. Don't recall his exact words, but he said that it represented his search for answers. He said something like 'It's the key to the mystery, to why we're here, what we're supposed to do.' A definite cliché response, but quite telling for him. He was undoubtedly a complicated guy, always struggling to find the clue to his happiness and wondering whether or not he measured up to his often-changing standards. Hell, I thought we were going to get married, and then he broke up with me for no apparent reason."

"So, what does it all mean?" asked Bill. "Are we supposed to connect the dots and come up with a reason why he committed suicide?"

"Perhaps we're overthinking this," Bob answered. "Jim wasn't necessarily leading us to answers as much as prompting us to share a few stories."

"Well, that's all fine," Bill said. "But shouldn't this good-looking, friendly, successful guy whom we all knew and loved have left a clue or two that he was about to swallow a bottle of pills?"

"I'm thinking that maybe he had gotten past the point of looking for someone who would talk him out of it," Jane said. "The pain was too great, the future too bleak. Plus, he probably didn't want to burden any of his closest friends with the secret—what he was contemplating."

They drank, toasted their missing guest, and told more stories for another two hours and then slowly began leaving the bar. Finally, only John and Janice remained. He put the five mementos back in the box.

John ordered another margarita. "You two were really engaged?"

"That's right," Janice answered. "Then one day Jim called and said that he didn't think we were marriage compatible, which I thought was an interesting word pairing. I asked him why and he said we should talk face-to-face. I was sick at the time and when I felt better a few days later, I drove to his apartment. But he had moved away without telling me. He finally sent me a letter to explain, but it didn't help much, although we still remained friends until yesterday."

"Unbelievable, but in hindsight, very much in character."

They were silent for several minutes and then John asked, "Now what?"

"How do you mean?"

"What to do with these things?"

Janice laughed. "I know. I'll take them and leave one at each of his favorite places. The marina, his favorite sports bar, maybe drop the ring in the campus wishing well where he proposed to me, and a few other spots. I think he would appreciate that."

John nodded. "Suppose so. But I still wish we knew why. There's got to be more to all of this."

"We'll be asking these questions forever. There is no good answer."

"That's not very comforting."

"No, it's not, but sometimes that's all there is—lots of memories, a few treasures and a box of ashes. We've likely just scratched the surface of the Jim Raymond mystery."

The bartender rang the last call bell, so John and Janice left the Good Friends Pub and went their separate ways.

The Leftovers

Austin Rice Jr. had traveled 300 miles, just so he could compare stories with his Fighting Eagles football teammates at their 25th high school reunion. More than 150 Sanctuary High School classmates and their spouses gathered in the grand ballroom of one of Santa Fe's oldest hotels.

It had been a difficult few years for Austin and his wife, and he looked forward to this "great escape," as Sally referred to the reunion. They sat at one of the two tables reserved for the "Conference Champions of 1993."

"This is quite a nice turnout," Austin said to Larry Montani, the star quarterback.

"More than last time. Hey, Austin, I heard you published a book of stories. What are they about?"

"Different things, such as two boys starting a fire, a fishing contest, someone searching for Bigfoot, and school bullying. Then there's one I wrote with you in mind. It's called A Wanted Man."

"Very funny. Maybe I'll get a copy."

Austin looked around the room. "You know, I can identify nearly all of the groups here. There is the band table, over there are the academics, then the glee club, the song girls and cheerleaders, social movers, a few theater people, and then, of course, us—the jocks. But there is one table I can't pinpoint. Over there, next to the bathrooms."

They turned to examine the table of 10 people crowded around the table.

"Don't recognize them," said Pat Boyle, their left tackle.

"Beats me," added former linebacker Johnny Stevens. "Wouldn't know them from Adam or anyone else."

"Maybe they're not Fighting Eagle grads, but rather wives, husbands, and others," Austin suggested.

They talked for another hour—about their last game, the wild Friday night parties, and their post-graduation successes. A few of the teammates were so drunk that they were already half asleep at their table.

"You know, I can't figure it out—who they are," Austin announced.

"Why do you even care?" Boyle asked.

Austin stood and said, "I suppose it's my writer's curiosity. I've got to find out."

He walked over to the table and sat in the one empty chair. They all stopped talking, waiting for Austin to introduce himself. After an awkward silence, he said, "Greetings, I'm Austin Rice, Jr., the defensive end who helped win the conference title in 1993. My teammates and I were not sure who you all are. Did you graduate from Sanctuary, or is this a spouses/significant others table?"

Their laughter got the attention of other alums.

"I told you this would happen," an attractive woman said quite loudly.

"What would happen?" Austin asked.

"That at least one of our fellow grads would wonder who the hell we are."

"Well, I meant no disrespect. But we were talking about

how we could identify everyone else in the room—band people, academics, social movers, and so on. And...."

"We are the ghosts," answered a woman wearing a Sanctuary High sweater.

"AKA the ignorables," another smiled.

"The invisibles."

"Unmentionables."

Finally, a tall, gray-haired man waved his left hand around the table and said, "Introducing the leftovers of Sanctuary High. You know, the ones you never saw, acknowledged, or fully appreciated. The group of otherwise good kids who just didn't fit into any one group, so, therefore, were isolated."

He waited for Austin to respond and then continued, "By the way, my name is Steve, that's John, and Jessica, Bonnie, Forrest, Becky, Lloyd, and Ben. We were all quite nice, friendly and interesting in our own way 25 years ago and still are."

A few of them smiled. A flustered Austin leaned back in his chair. Never an eloquent speaker, he now could barely form a complete sentence.

"Look. I just thought...was curious about...wondered if...oh, crap..."

"Very well put," Steve said. He moved closer to Austin and whispered: "You don't remember, do you?"

Austin's silence and puzzled expression confirmed his ignorance. The others had turned away, once again engaged in their own conversations. But Steve was intrigued.

"Remember what?"

"That you were one of us."

"How do you mean? I was not."

Steve shrugged his shoulders. "Sure, I remember you as a nervous, depressed ninth grader who couldn't find his place. You often sat at our lunchroom table or by yourself. I recall exchanging a few words with you. You were also one of the school ghosts. Seemed pretty miserable and alone. Then you started playing football, at which you were obviously quite good. After that, you ignored us."

Austin shook his head. "I honestly don't think I would have been that shallow."

"Look, I'm not saying you were intentionally rude or didn't like us," Steve continued. "Freshman year is a miserable time for many young people; trying to figure out where we fit in and such. And, I must emphasize that we are partly responsible for being leftovers. Some seem to embrace the aloneness."

Austin stood and held out his right hand. "You must be thinking of someone else. But I've enjoyed talking with you."

"Sure, our memories do get fuzzy as we age. Anyway, enjoy your reunion."

Austin went to the bar and ordered two drinks. "Could I have been a leftover back then? I just don't see it."

"What was that?" the bartender asked.

"Nothing. Just talking out loud."

Austin walked to the memory table that included a display of faded black and white photos and yearbooks from each of their four years at Sanctuary High. He found the 1990 edition and quickly flipped the pages to find his photo. He stared at the unsmiling 15-year-old, nervously posing for the photographer during the first week of school.

I remember that day; it was soon after he said they were

getting a divorce. Nothing was the same after that. Just a blur of unhappiness…until I started running again.

Austin had spent every afternoon racing around the school track, until the football coach encouraged him to try out for the junior varsity team.

"Austin, what's the matter? What are you doing?" He looked up and saw Sally standing next to him. Austin pushed the yearbooks aside. "I guess I was lost in thought," he said.

"There has been a lot of that lately. It's time we talked about something."

Austin pointed to the chair next to him. "Sit down. What is it?"

"This is difficult to ask, but I'll try. Do you still blame me for that night with Frank Darnell?"

Austin was breathing heavily. They had never discussed the incident before.

"How did…"

"How did I find out that you thought I had slept with him? I was cleaning our hall closet last week and found the journal with your notes about the writing trips with Frank. You made several references to his big mistake and one comment he allegedly made about spending the night with me. That was the last note, and then soon after you stopped working with him. It seemed clear that you were angry then and have been ever since. And I was the only one who really knew what had happened."

"What do you mean?"

"Austin, we never slept together, which is obviously what you believed. We were all drunk after their wedding rehearsal dinner, you and I had argued, and he was trying to comfort me. We were in his room talking and he suddenly passed out, so I left. I guess you got the idea that he had been with a woman and later confronted him. He must have imagined it was me because I had been in his room. Fact is, he was in no condition to have had sex with another woman that night."

Austin's face was flushed, and his hands shook.

"My God. I can't believe this. I thought he had and used it against him after we had started working on the book. When he said it had been you, I didn't believe him at first but then for some reason wasn't sure. So, I now have you at the top of my list of those to make amends to, with him being a very close second."

"Fine, I accept your apology for being such a colossal, mistrusting jerk who has made both of our lives miserable for the last year. You can start making up for it next week. Right now, we should get back to the others."

When he returned to the football table, Austin's teammates were waiting for an explanation.

"Okay, give it up," Boyle said. "Who are they? What did you find out?"

Austin was still shaken from his conversation with Sally, so she prompted him. "They were classmates, right Austin?"

"Yes, they are a group of our fellow grads...rather nice people," he said slowly. "They reminded me how high school can be a metaphor for life."

"A what?" Montani wondered.

"Well, the point is that high school gives us some of the starter tools to be an adult, but it's up to us to put them to work, to continue learning, understanding, and improving ourselves, something I haven't always done."

"I think you've turned out reasonably well," Boyle said.

"Okay, but I've definitely made some missteps. I'm obviously not done learning and growing."

Montani stirred his drink and said, "You're quite the philosopher tonight, Austin. You should write a story or even a novel about the reunion and all of us. Feel free to use my name, as long as I'm a sympathetic character. You know, the strong, heroic type."

Austin glanced at Sally, who smiled. "I'll keep that in mind. Perhaps I will write that book. Could call it The Great American Reunion. What do you think?"

Several of his teammates nodded in agreement and Austin began outlining the book on the back of his Sanctuary High reunion program.

Contact David

If you have a question or suggestion for David Robinson,
please write him at davidlrob123@gmail.com
Also, to learn more about David and his future
stories, visit www.dlrstories.wordpress.com

Printed in the United States
By Bookmasters